A SHIVER OF WONDER

C. S. Lewis

A SHIVER OF WONDER

DERICK BINGHAM

AMBASSADOR INTERNATIONAL
Greenville, South Carolina • Belfast, Northern Ireland

C. S. Lewis:
A Shiver of Wonder

Printed in the United States of America

British spelling used throughout.

ISBN 1 932307 32 X

Published by the Ambassador Group

Ambassador Emerald International
427 Wade Hampton Blvd.
Greenville, SC 29609
USA
www.emeraldhouse.com

and

Ambassador Publications Ltd.
Providence House
Ardenlee Street
Belfast BT6 8QJ
Northern Ireland
www.ambassador-productions.com

The colophon is a trademark of Ambassador

For Peter McConkey, chef *extraordinaire*, who pointed
me back to writing this book; and for Adrian Adger,
who gently and faithfully prayed it through.

Whether we were his pupils in the classroom or no, we are all his pupils, and we shall not look upon his like again.[1]

DAME HELEN GARDNER,
writing about C. S. Lewis

I stand on the windy uplands among the hills of Down
With all the world spread out beneath,
Meadow and sea and town,
And ploughlands on the far-off hills
That glow with friendly brown.

And ever across the rolling land to the far horizon line,
Where the blue hills border the misty west,
I see the white roads twine,
The rare roads and the fair roads
That call this heart of mine.

I see them dip in the valleys and
Vanish and rise and bend
From shadowy dell to windswept fell,
And still to the West they wend,
And over the cold blue ridge at last
To the great world's uttermost end.

And the call of the roads is upon me,
A desire in my spirit has grown
To wander forth in the highways,
'Twixt earth and sky alone,
And seek for the lands no foot has trod
And the seas no sail has known....

"The Roads," taken from *Spirits of Bondage, A Cycle of Lyrics,* written by C. S. Lewis under the pseudonym Clive Hamilton. The book was published by Heinneman in 1919, when Lewis was just twenty-one years of age, and reveals his early giftedness as a poet.

These verses show C. S. Lewis's deep and, as it turned out, lifelong love for County Down. He once described his idea of Heaven to his friend David Bleakley as "Oxford lifted and placed in the middle of the County Down"!

TABLE OF CONTENTS

PREFACE

The older gentleman approached me quietly. He wore tweeds and, speaking gently, he asked me to lunch. He said his name was Bishop Arthur Goodwin-Hudson. As I had never had lunch with an Anglican Bishop before, I wondered what was coming. He had heard me speak on the Scriptures, and now he wanted to talk to me.

When eventually we settled down to lunch together, his opening phrase intrigued me: "We have something in common," he said, in a kindly way. I immediately perked up. "You and I are interested in 'the man on the outside.'"[2] It touched me that he had noticed, for, in truth, when communicating on Christian matters, I have tried to be mindful that my listeners or readers may not be familiar with what I am talking about.

Picking up on Christ's analogy that evangelism is like fishing, the Bishop told me that his "fishing boat" had been the Anglican Church. During the Second World War, when he was a much younger Anglican minister, he had approached the outstanding Christian industrialist and film producer J. Arthur Rank, who sat on the board of Odeon Cinemas. The Bishop asked him if he could have permission to bring a Christian message to the soldiers who attended the Sunday evening film at the Odeon Cinema in London. Rank said yes, but the manager of the cinema was much harder to persuade. He warned that the soldiers could give a minister a very rough time indeed. Eventually, however, Arthur managed to persuade the manager to let him speak. The first person to be converted to Christ was the cinema manager himself!

My new acquaintance began to expand on the theme of the importance of reaching "the man on the outside," the person who has little or no knowledge of the Christian faith. He told me that when he was in the United States he had heard what he called a "raw young preacher," who wore loud ties, but who had something special. With the Bishop of Barking and others, he invited this dairy farmer's son from North Carolina to Harringay Arena in London to preach the gospel. "The Christians tore him apart," the Bishop said, looking me straight in the eye; "but the sinners loved him." In fact, by the Saturday night of the first week, 11,400 people had filled the Harringay Arena to capacity, and 30,000 more were standing outside. Landline relays were set up, and 400,000 listeners received the audio signal from the services via the 400 lines that went out from Harringay.[3]

In this year of writing, it is the fiftieth anniversary of that twelve-week Billy Graham London Crusade. A significant book could be written of the stories of people whose lives were changed by Christ at that pivotal time in the spiritual life of a nation.

The Bishop then shared with me some of his experiences serving Christ in Chatham during the Second World War. His ministry was challenged in a unique way when he received an interesting request from an Ulsterman. Maybe it was his affinity with that Ulsterman that led him so generously to invite me to lunch that day in England twenty-three years ago; I would like to think so. Maybe the Bishop was kind to me because of his affection for that Ulsterman; the name of the Ulsterman was Clive Staples Lewis.

In the winter of 1941, C. S. Lewis received an invitation from the RAF's Commander-in-Chief, the Reverend Maurice Edwards' to address the Royal Air Force. This invitation followed the incredible success of Lewis's BBC wartime broadcasts. Lewis offered to conduct lectures during weekends.

It was a year of many great crises across the nation and the world. In Britain, the popular vocabulary for the year 1941 was full of such words as dictator, infamy, arsenal, casualties, avenge, treacherous, potent, uncanny, indomitable. It was the year that 180 German bombers dropped 203 metric tons of bombs and 800 firebomb canisters on the City of Belfast in one night. On two nights in March, 200 planes pounded Clydebank in Glasgow for fifteen hours. In North Shields, at midnight on 3 May, a single bomb from a lone German raider scored a direct hit on a public air raid shelter beneath Wilkinson's lemonade factory. One hundred and three lives were lost, many of them women and children. Though hardened by the horrors of nine months of the Blitz, Londoners were shaken on 11 May by a horrendous raid. In brilliant moonlight, 550 German planes indiscriminately dropped hundreds of high-explosive bombs and 100,000 incendiaries. In June 1941, Hitler invaded the Soviet Union; and in December Japan's attack on Pearl Harbour provoked the war in the Pacific. The Fuehrer had ordered the physical extermination of the Jewish people. The year 1941 saw that order being unrelentingly and savagely carried out across Europe.

Under such conditions, and in such an atmosphere, C. S. Lewis set patiently about his work of sowing Christian seed. For years he traveled all over the country in crowded trains. In the summer, particularly, he journeyed from the Highlands of Perthshire to the mountains of Wales, seeking to win airmen for Christ. The Bishop told me that Lewis was deeply concerned for the spiritual wellbeing of aircrews going out to die, so he invited the Bishop to join him as a speaker on his lecture tours. "I'll go for their heads," said Lewis; "you go for their hearts."

Lewis believed that Hitler was not the only enemy in Europe. He believed there were other anti-Christian forces at work. In fact, they had been at work for some considerable time, rooted particularly in David Hume's eighteenth-century view that we live in an empty, godless universe, devoid of purpose. Kant's belief that concepts such as God, the soul, and immortality belong to the realm of the unknowable, and Darwin's belief that theology has no place in a scientific outlook, had added to the increase of unbelief. The theories of Marx and Engels had captivated millions and driven them away from Christianity. "God's Funeral", as Thomas Hardy metaphorically called the decline in Christian belief, seemed to have taken place. Interestingly, though, this famous poem does not mock believers. It sympathises with them, and, in my opinion, expresses envy toward them. Wistfully, Hardy remembers his earlier, now discarded belief:

How sweet it was in years far hied
To start the wheels of day with trustful prayer,
To lie down liegely at the eventide
And feel a blest assurance he was there!

And who or what shall fill his place?
Whither will wanderers turn distracted eyes
For some fixed star to stimulate their pace
Towards the goal of their enterprise?…

Some in the background then I saw,
Sweet women, youths, men, all incredulous,
Who chimed as one: "This is a counterfeit of straw,
This requiem mockery! Still he lives to us!"
I could not buoy their faith: and yet

> *Many I had known: with all I sympathised;*
> *And though struck speechless I did not forget,*
> *That what was mourned for, I too, once had prized.*[4]

One day Hardy was found with college dons, discussing the ceremony by which he would be sworn into an honorary fellowship at Magdalene College, Cambridge. In the conversation, he pointed out that he used to attend church three times on a Sunday; he also revealed that he had a lot of knowledge of ecclesiastical music. "Of course, it's only sentimental to me now," he said.[5]

Since Hardy's time many more millions of people in Western Europe had been discarding Christianity. Now, at the height of the Second World War, God raised up a unique apologist to stir the thinking of those men, women, and young people on the outside of Christian belief. Interestingly, in 1955, Lewis took up residence in Magdalene College, Cambridge as the Professor of Medieval and Renaissance English.

Unashamedly Lewis believed in evangelism and in the fact that he was a Christian apologist. He wrote as follows:

> Where a speaker has that gift, the direct evangelical appeal of the "Come to Jesus type" can be as overwhelming today as it was 100 years ago....I cannot do it: but those who can ought to do it with all their might. I am not sure that the ideal Missionary team ought not to consist of one who argues and one who (in the fullest sense of the word) preaches. Put up your arguer first to undermine their intellectual prejudices; then let the evangelist proper launch his appeal.[6]

How successful was Lewis's Christian work for the Royal Air Force? The truth is that often no one turned up. Sometimes fewer than a dozen men came. It was better at the bigger stations, where men of real intellectual ability were in his audiences. "It is fair to say," wrote his friend George Sayer, "he made impression on only a few." [7] And this was the man who had just addressed millions so effectively across the nation by radio. Christian work has its challenges; but then a grain of wheat needs first to fall into the ground and die, or it abides alone. Winter snows cover the seeds; biting winds blow over them, and there is not a sign of stirring until spring. Then the harvest day is assured.

Working as an academic at Oxford University, Lewis's work as a Christian apologist knew many a chilling wind. Even when dining at his college he tended to feel increasingly isolated, because the open expression of his Christian views made him many enemies. It was thought that a man's belief was a private affair and should not be written about or published. The academic who wrote from a Christian perspective for children was not given any encouragement. For some, the fact that he sought to see others converted to Christ was quite unforgivable. The academics who held a naturalistic point of view were ranged against him. C. S. Lewis's faith and courage came at huge personal cost. He stood up for Christ, and he bore the scars.

Now, the springtime for the seed that Lewis sowed has come. Currently, there are tens of millions of copies of his books in circulation in many different translations. For example, *The Chronicles of Narnia* has been translated into Afrikaans, Chinese, Danish, Greek, Icelandic, Russian, Slovene, and Welsh. "The man on the outside" is listening to him as never before. In the United States, C. S. Lewis's books have become one of the most potent forces for Christianity in the nation.

Walden Media has engaged the highly acclaimed director Andrew Adamson, best known for his animated feature *Shrek*, to direct the first live-action feature film adaptation of Lewis's children's book, *The Lion, the Witch and the Wardrobe*. This is expected to be the first of five films based on Lewis's Narnia books. The filming is taking place in the forests, high country, and coastal areas of New Zealand's South Island. "Narnia was such a vivid and real world to me as a child," Adamson states, "as it is to millions of fans." I share Walden's excitement in giving those fans an epic theatrical experience worthy of their imaginations, and driving a new generation toward the works of C. S. Lewis. "Making a film that crosses generations is a far easier task when the source material resonates with such themes as truth, loyalty, and belief in something greater than yourself." [8]

The variety of lives touched by Lewis's life and ministry is staggering. At this point, though, let me concentrate on just one of those lives. For over three decades, on both sides of the Atlantic, Kenneth Tynan was the hot centre of the theatre and film worlds. Arguably he was the greatest theatre critic of the twentieth century, and at one period of his life he was the Literary Manager at the National Theatre in London. He was generally perceived to be a notorious eccentric, a sexual obsessive, a womaniser, an atheist, and a champagne socialist.

When Kenneth Tynan's diaries were published by Bloomsbury, though, a very different side of him emerged. They reveal a man who was overwhelmed by melancholy and self-loathing. There was a desperate emptiness at the heart of his life. An ailing hedonist, he died of emphysema. A look into his diaries reveals a haunting thread of commentary about C. S. Lewis, his tutor at Magdalen College in Oxford.

He writes that, while at Oxford in 1948, his girlfriend jilted him on the eve of what was to have been their marriage. He went to Lewis in despair, asking if he could postpone his final examinations until Christmas. Lewis immediately agreed, and "got me with the Christian business of consolation." Lewis reminded Tynan of a story he had once told him of how he had been a hair's breadth from death during a German bombing raid in his home city of Birmingham. Gently, Lewis pointed out to Tynan that if the wind had blown the bomb a few inches nearer his house he would already have been dead for eight years, and that "every moment of life since then had been a bonus, a tremendous free gift, a present that only the blackest ingratitude could refuse."

Tynan writes, "As I listened to him, my problems began to dwindle to their proper proportions: I had entered his room suicidal and I left exhilarated." He notes that Lewis was a "deeply kind and charitable man," and that, because Tynan stammered, Lewis "kindly undertook to read my weekly essays aloud for me....[T]he prospect of hearing my words pronounced in that wonderfully juicy and judicious voice had a permanently disciplining effect on my prose style." Tynan notes, "If ever I were to stray into the Christian camp, it would be because of Lewis's arguments as expressed in books like *Miracles*. (He never intruded them into tutorials)."[9] Tynan calls Lewis "the great Christian persuader," a man who is "brilliant and provocative."[10]

On 4 April 1971 he writes, "I read *That Hideous Strength* and once more the old tug reasserts itself—a tug of genuine war with my recent self. How thrilling he makes goodness seem—how tangible and radiant!" Tynan explains that he is struggling with whether he should write a film he has been asked to write and direct. "To do this work may well be a wicked act," he muses; "Am I being tempted with sin, or tested with the chance of committing myself to responsible work?"[11] On 6 December 1974 he wonders if Lewis will finally guide him back to belief.

While reading Lewis's *Reflections on the Psalms,* Tynan notes, on 27 April 1976, that C. S. Lewis "would certainly hold the view that, by drawing my attention to this passage in his book, God was offering me yet another signpost pointing towards acceptance of the Christian faith."[12] Kenneth Tynan hoped that when he died he would be buried as close to Lewis as possible. It must have been truly a poignant moment when his ashes were buried in the churchyard of St. Cross in Oxford, and his daughter Roxana read a passage from Lewis's sermon The Weight of Glory. It was a passage warning that, when we think beauty is located in music or books, they betray us. What comes through them is, in fact, longing. If we mistake them for the thing itself, they become idols in our lives that will break our hearts. The passage teaches that the beauty we perceive is only an echo, a scent, and news of a greater thing.

It seems to me that, through Lewis's writing, Kenneth Tynan had felt a shiver of wonder at things which the world, the flesh, and the devil could never match or deliver. Few who have read Lewis's work have not had a similar shiver. Tynan had read the majestic essay Lewis wrote on The Incarnation in his book *Miracles*, one of the greatest defences of the deity of Christ in literature. He had read of our righteousnesses' being as filthy rags, but of redemption made possible through Christ, and of a coming new heaven and new earth. But he had made a choice in his life, and what he chased did not satisfy the longings of his soul. Tynan's diaries reveal a heart and mind touched by the work of the great Christian apologist, and challenged by the Christian gospel. He is a microcosm of "the man on the outside" that Lewis was always trying to reach for Christ.

At the time of Lewis's centenary in 1998, The Sunday *Times* carried a full-page feature of an extract from the section on pride in *Mere Christianity*. The feature contained a picture of the book as well as a photo of the founder of Domino's Pizza, Thomas

Monaghan. The article bore one of the longest headlines ever to appear in the newspaper. It read, "This man is a pizza millionaire. He's smiling because he is giving £600m to charity and devoting himself to God. He is doing so because he read this book by C. S. Lewis." The feature then points out that, after reading Lewis's analysis of pride in *Mere Christianity*, Monaghan decided to sell his Rolls Royce and Bentley limousines, his yacht, his private helicopter, his collection of Frank Lloyd Wright artefacts, and most of his shares in Domino's Pizza.

In her autobiography, *The Path to Power*, Margaret Thatcher devotes at least three pages to Lewis's influence on her life. "It was the religious writing of that High Anglican C. S. Lewis which had most impact upon my intellectual religious formation," she says.

> The power of his broadcasts, sermons, and essays came from a combination of simple language with theological depth. Who has ever portrayed more wittingly and convincingly the way in which Evil works on our human weaknesses than he did in *The Screwtape Letters*? Who has ever made more accessible the profound concepts of Natural Law than he did in *The Abolition of Man* and in the opening passages of *Mere Christianity*? I remember most clearly the impact on me of *Christian Behaviour* (republished in *Mere Christianity*, but originally appearing as radio talks). This went to the heart of the appalling disparity between the way in which we Christians behave and the ideals we profess.[13]

To Gerry Haliwell and Peter Mandelson, to Liam Gallagher and J. R. R. Tolkien, to Charles Colson and Pope John Paul II, and to millions of other people besides, aspects of Lewis's life and work have proved helpful and inspiring. In a recent BBC TV documentary, Ian Paisley Jr. was sitting in Lewis's Parish Church, speaking with appreciation of his writing and life.

On 21 July 1998 the Royal Mail issued a series of special centenary stamps, entitled "Magical Worlds," featuring *The Lion, the Witch and the Wardrobe*. A musical portrait of Lewis's life also toured Britain during that year. Even Hamley's, England's most famous toy shop, hosted a special one-hundredth birthday party in honour of C. S. Lewis. These are significant outward signs that this apologist still has an audience. The more important inward signs have been seen in the incredible number of people who have become Christians through reading his work. Here in Ulster, I think of the gifted evangelist and Bible teacher Michael Perrott, who was converted from agnosticism to Christ through reading *Mere Christianity*. To this day he prizes a letter he received from C. S. Lewis following his conversion.

The list of those Lewis has influenced continues to increase. Recently I was on the thirty-second floor of a Japanese hotel in downtown Tokyo. I went down to a little shop on the ground floor to buy an English newspaper. There, in the land of thirty million gods, I noticed a little pile of books. It was *The Chronicles of Narnia* in Japanese. People "on the outside" are obviously still taking serious note of this unique and gifted Ulsterman. I smiled in my heart and went back with relish to my work of preaching, teaching, and writing about the Christian faith, encouraged that Christian seed brings an amazing harvest.

A friend of mine who is not a Christian believer was having a coffee with me. He and his girlfriend had been watching a BBC production of *The Lion, the Witch and the Wardrobe*. He suddenly turned to me and emphasised how his girlfriend "had really liked the lion." I pointed out to my non-believing friend the Christly nature of the King of Narnia. Lewis wrote that there hung about the mane of Aslan, the High King above all kings, "some strange and solemn perfume."[11] To all who have come to know Him, this is an apposite description of Jesus Christ. To them, *His name is as ointment poured forth; His love is better than wine, and the scent of His perfumes than all spices.*[12] That perfume touched the life of C. S. Lewis in his day; it touches us in ours, and it will touch incalculable multitudes of the redeemed forever. Following our conversation, my non-believing friend kindly purchased cinema tickets as a gift for my wife and me to see the film *Shadowlands,* which he subsequently went to see for himself!

Recently, the English comedienne Ronni Ancona championed *The Lion, the Witch and the Wardrobe* on the BBC's "The Big Read." This was a television programme which asked people in the United Kingdom to choose their favourite book of the twentieth century. Various people championed a range of authors. I thought Ronni's defence was articulate, passionate, and courageously up-front about the Christian content of Lewis's work. She said you might as well criticise a baker for using yeast in his dough as criticise Lewis for the Christian content of his work! It was part of him. Well said, Ronni; well said!

As I was nearing the completion of this biography, I asked Dr. Stuart Briscoe what he thought of C. S. Lewis. Stuart is a well-known speaker and Minister-at-Large of the approximately ten-thousand-member Elmbrook Church in Brookfield, Wisconsin, USA. He has written more than forty books, and has had the privilege of preaching to hundreds of thousands of people across a hundred countries around the world. This is his moving response:

> The writings of C. S. Lewis have been a source of delight and enrichment to me for many years. Unlike many avid Lewis readers, I was not introduced to him as a child, and was not reared on Narnia. It was when I began to do a little preaching at the tender age of 17, and shortly thereafter embarked on a lifetime involvement in young people's ministry, that I began to draw heavily on his apologetic arguments. His treatment of

thorny issues, such as the problem of pain, appealed greatly to me and to the sceptical young people who abounded in the bars and coffee bars of the British Isles. I remember many a young person, who wanted to dismiss Jesus as another good man, being brought up short by Lewis's insistence that this was not an option; because, if Jesus was not who He said He was—the Christ—then He was either a crook or crazy. But Lewis put it in such a way that even those who were defeated by his arguments had to laugh when Lewis, instead of saying Jesus would have to be crazy, suggested he would be similar to a man who thought he was a poached egg!

In later years I was greatly impressed by his ideas about "joy" or "*sehnsucht,*" and particularly by his explanation that [since] even the most satisfying things in life fail to satisfy completely[,]...we must have been made for another world. I have found people all over the world who can relate to this insight and respond to its challenge.

In more recent times, I have found his writings on worship of great value[s] particularly in light of what are now being called "Worship Wars." I love his candour in explaining the time when he did not like God very much because His insistence on being worshipped seemed rather like a vain woman who thrives on compliments! But God's desire for our worship led him to realise that worship is not for God's benefit but ours! That set me off on deep thinking about the reality of worship.

And in recent days I have benefited greatly from a reading of *The Question of God* by Dr. Armand M. Nicholi, in which Lewis's powerful arguments against Freudian philosophy are laid out in compelling and relevant fashion. Lewis still speaks today!

I don't know what I would have done without him.

So, from Prime Ministers to World War II pilots, from art critics to Japanese children, from billionaires to bishops and a huge variety of people in between, millions of individuals from all kinds of corners across the world have been, and are continuing to be, influenced by C. S. Lewis.

Sadly, it turned out that I never saw Bishop Goodwin-Hudson again. Research tells me "Arthur William Goodwin-Hudson was assistant Bishop of Sydney 1960-65, and Dean of Sydney 1962-65. On returning to England, he was incumbent of St. Paul's, Portman Square 1965-78. He died 17th September 1985 in England."

As I now turn with deep affection to write a life of C. S. Lewis, in my mind's eye I can still see A. W. Goodwin-Hudson. There he sits at the other side of the table, four years before his death, gentle and courteous, talking to me about his friend C. S. Lewis and the subject of reaching "the man on the outside." The encounter makes me think about a recent conversation I had at Barr Hall near Portaferry in County Down, with Miguel Mesquita da Cunha who is a political advisor to the President of the European Commission. We talked about how Lewis was once "*on* the outside" himself. Said Miguel, we can now call him "the man *from* the outside." This is a vitally important distinction. Significantly by God's grace he came inside God's kingdom, and wrote about it in a way that few others have ever done.

This book is about that journey and its international and eternal consequences.

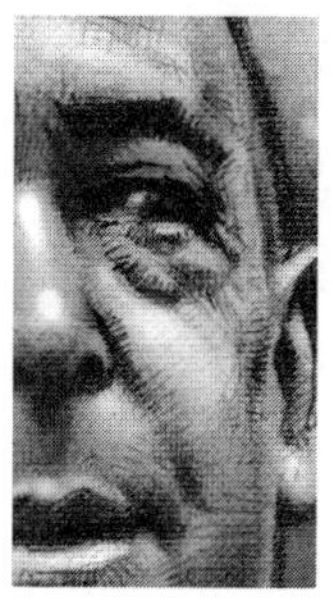

Chapter One

THE LOST ADDRESS

Of all months, April is probably the best loved in Western Europe. Shakespeare wrote of "proud-pied April, dressed in all his trim." The skies in April are bluer, and there is such a "clear shining after rain."[1] In April the songs the birds sing with their wings still wet sound more joyous than any other songs. There is a proliferation of tulips and forget-me-nots, blushing daisies and snowy blackthorns.

On the island of Ireland, the green foliage of tree and hedge is almost intoxicating in April; virtually every shade of green can be found. All across the country buds are swelling, and fresh molehills show that Mr. Mole is again spring-cleaning. Young rabbits speed across the meadows. In sleepy gardens bees swarm from their hives, and whole columns of whirling wings can be seen rising and falling. It is the month when the swallows return from Africa and set about the very hard work of nest building from the very moment they arrive. They mend their old nests and can be seen setting the foundations of new ones.

In the Ireland of April 1905, the swallows were not the only ones busy building new homes. A little family had just moved into their new residence in the suburbs of Belfast. They gave their home the name Little Lea. Earlier that year there was a notice in the *Belfast and Province of Ulster Directory*:

> Circular Road. Strandtown. Off Holywood Road. Rt. hand side. New house in course of erection for A. J. Lewis, Solicitor.[2]

The details given in the *Directory* of Mr. Lewis's neighbours, in the immediate and wider vicinity of his new home, display a microcosm of Irish society just following the close of the Victorian era. We find Mr. Sam Quillan, gardener, at Lakeview Cottage; Mr. W. Masterson, tea merchant, at Ballymisert House; Mr. William H. Patterson, ironmonger, at Garranard; Robert Symington, coachman, at Glenfarlough Cottages. At Bernagh lives Joshua M. Greeves, millowner; Mr. Thomas Rice, the stationmaster, looks after the local Tillysburn Railway Station.

Moving a little farther away from the new house being built for the Lewis family, we find Sir W. G. Ewart living at Glenmachan House. Amongst others living at Glenmachan Cottages there is a labourer, a meter inspector, a groom, a land steward, and a ploughman. Col. McCance lives at Knocknagoney House, and W. Davis, a coachman, lives at Knocknagoney House Lodge. At Ormiston Buildings, we find a ship carpenter, a tobacconist, a druggist, a hairdresser, a plumber, a gas fitter, a draper, and a boat merchant.

Even in 1905 the wider City of Belfast had moved a long way from its origins. Its name is derived from the words *beol*, meaning "ford," and *fearsad*, meaning "sandbank." The first recorded account of the building of ships in Belfast appeared in the year 1636, when the Presbyterian clergyman of Belfast built a vessel of

150 tons' register. More recently, Harland & Wolfe had launched the *Oceanic*, then the largest ship on earth. "In the years running up to the Great War, citizens could boast that their City had the greatest shipyard, rope works, tobacco factory, linen spinning mill, dry dock, and tea-machinery works in the world."[3] The city was justly considered to be the commercial metropolis of Ireland.

Albert James Lewis, a Police Court Solicitor, whose father had emigrated from Wales to Ireland, was educated at Lurgan College in the beautiful "Orchard County" of Ireland, the County of Armagh. A local brewer, Samuel Watts, had left an endowment for the building of a school that would provide an "English classical and agricultural education." The second Headmaster of that school was Mr. W. T. Kirkpatrick, who came to Lurgan College from the Royal Belfast Academical Institution in 1875. His influence was to reach far beyond the newly established and flourishing school on Lurgan's College Walk. Besides having Albert Lewis under his care at Lurgan College from 1877 to 1879, Kirkpatrick was to become his lifelong friend and a tutor to his son Clive. On retirement from the school, Kirkpatrick was to have Clive at his home in Great Bookham in Surrey to prepare him for entrance examinations to Oxford University. He was to teach Clive his mother's formidable gift of logic, to devastating effect. Albert's Welsh temperament—full of rhetoric, passion, and sentiment—could easily be moved to anger and just as easily to tenderness. Laughter and tears played a large part in his life, but happiness was not a dominant feature. He was a kind and generous man, possessing an excellent memory and a very quick mind. He had a deep, clear, ringing voice, and exuded a considerable presence.

Albert was a brilliant and skillful teller of short, entertaining stories about real incidents or people. He could act all the characters in his stories. He loved poetry that contained pathos and rhetoric; this significant literary streak, being encouraged by his Headmaster, led Albert to write his own stories and poetry. He loved the liturgy of the Church of Ireland as contained in its Prayer Book, and he loved the infinite treasures found in the verbal vaults of the Bible. With these gifts and interests, it is not surprising that he was the first Superintendent of the Sunday School at St. Mark's, Dundela, a nearby Belfast suburb. Albert's law practise was at 83 Royal Avenue, and he was to become Sessional Solicitor of the Belfast City Council and the Belfast and County Down Railway Company, as well as Solicitor to the National Society for the Prevention of Cruelty to Children. He impressed many juries with his effective speaking abilities, and he also gave his services as a speaker to the Conservative Party, gaining frequent acclaim from newspapers for his efforts. He loved to read Anthony Trollope's political novels. Later both his boys claimed that, given the freedom and the resources, he would have made a significant politician.

Through his love for literature, Albert came to meet the love of his life. It is said that a faint heart has never won a fair lady. His heart had been stirred by the Rector's pale, fair-haired, blue-eyed daughter, Florence Augusta (Flora) Hamilton, but her love was difficult to win. Flora was born at Queenstown in County Cork in 1862 and as a young girl lived in Rome with her parents. She proved to be of a much cooler temperament than her father, who was a chaplain in the Royal Navy during the whole of the Crimean War and a chaplain of the Anglican Holy Trinity Church in Rome from 1870 to 1874. The Hamiltons were the descendants of a titled Scottish family that was allowed to take land in County Down in the reign of James I. The Reverend Hamilton was a very highly principled and emotionally charged man. We are told that he frequently wept in his pulpit. It must have caused him and his family great sadness that he had to spend much of his short life in a mental hospital. It seems that he suffered from scant praise. Yet surely a man is not without memorable significance who willingly served in the Crimea and, in fact, volunteered for duty in camps where death from cholera occurred every single day. Perhaps he saw things that others of us will never see. Let his Maker be his judge.

So, Thomas Hamilton was the first Rector of St. Mark's, Dundela, ministering there from 1874 to 1900. His wife, Mary, was a liberal in politics, an enthusiastic feminist, a supporter of the suffragettes, and a Home Ruler. (A Home Ruler was a person who believed that Ireland should be self-governed but still remain part of the British Empire.) She was a committed vegetarian and a cat collector, and she kept an extremely untidy and disorganised rectory! Mary Warren Hamilton came from an Anglo-Norman family planted in Ireland in the reign of Henry II. She was an extremely political animal indeed, and very intelligent with it.

Mary Hamilton's daughter, Florence, known as Flora, is of great significance in any study of the life of C. S. Lewis. She was to have a profound influence upon him, even though she died when he was only ten years of age, leaving him horrendously bereft. She had a great gift that she would pass on to him: a mind that thought distinctly and logically.

Between 1881 and 1885 Flora attended ladies' classes at Methodist College, Belfast, and, at the same time, the Royal University of Ireland, now known as Queen's University. The University's beautiful main college building, designed by Charles Lanyon, is modelled on Magdalen College, Oxford, where Flora's son would achieve great fame. Nearby, stretching across seventeen acres, are the beautiful Royal Botanical Gardens, with their lawn, Teak Ground, Yew Ground, and Hawthorn Collection.

The Ornamental Water, the Fernery, and the famous Palm House conservatory enhance all of these grounds.

Queen's University is nowadays famous for its major contribution to world medicine and engineering. In Flora Hamilton's time the Maths Department had a significant reputation. Flora read Mathematics and Logic. In her first public exam in 1880, she got a first in Geometry and Algebra, and in her finals in 1881, a first in Logic and a second-class honours degree in Mathematics. She took a B.A. in 1886.

With regard to Mathematics, Flora was extraordinary, and many regarded her as a bit of a bluestocking. Perhaps in her time a more prevalent Ulster view of mathematics was that of Mother Goose:

Multiplication is a vexation,
Division's twice as bad;
The rule of three perplexes me,
And practise makes me mad!

Another unusual aspect in Flora's make-up was a deep love of literature; few mathematicians carry such a trait. A voracious reader of good novels, Flora saw one of her own stories, "The Princess Rosetta," published in *The Household Journal of London* in 1889.

Albert's brother, William, had first courted Florence, but she turned him down, telling him she could never love him. From the beginning Albert had to approach Flora very carefully indeed. When he proposed to her in 1886, she offered him only friendship. By now devoted to her, Albert exploited their love of literature as a major link between them. Flora used him as a sounding board for her short stories and articles, and over the seven years following the proposal they wrote many letters to each other. It took a long time to win Flora's love; but her friendship with Albert began to shift to a fondness for him, and eventually she woke up to the fact that she would be deeply unhappy if they parted. Her feelings for him were deeper than she outwardly demonstrated. Even at the time of their engagement in June 1893, she admitted to him that she was not sure if she loved him, but she was sure that she could not bear not seeing him. So, on 29 August 1894, the pale, gifted, cool-headed, blue-eyed mathematician and the somewhat tempestuous lawyer were married at St. Mark's, Dundela. They honeymooned in North Wales and moved into Dundela Villas in East Belfast. It was a marriage that was to be marked by deep devotion from each partner. Warren Hamilton Lewis was born on 16 June 1895; and three years later, on 29 November 1898, Clive Staples Lewis was born.

In looking at the childhood of C. S. Lewis, all kinds of threads combine to make up the intriguing tapestry that will emerge. It was William Wordsworth who wrote, "the child is the father of the man"; and looking back on his own childhood, he wrote in a section of *The Prelude*:

There was a boy, ye knew him well, ye Cliffs
And Islands off Winander! Many a time
At evening, when the stars had just begun
To move along the edges of the hills,
Rising or setting, would he stand alone
Beneath the trees, or by the glimmering lake,
And there, with fingers interwoven, both hands
Press'd closely, palm to palm, and to his mouth
Uplifted, he, as through an instrument
Blew mimic hootings to the silent owls
That they might answer him. And they would shout

Across the watery Vale, and shout again,
Responsive to his call, with quivering peals.

It is not the fells and water of the beautiful Lake District that touch the very young C. S. Lewis, but a little town called Castlerock in the northwest corner of Northern Ireland. The middle classes of the time, and in particular the middle classes of Belfast, took their children to the seaside for two or three months of the summer. The thinking behind this practise was that fever such as typhoid (an infectious bacterial disease) was more common in the warm weather of the summer than in other seasons. The year before Clive was born, typhoid had affected 27,000 people.

Over many years, the Lewises were to take a furnished house at Castlerock during the summer months. Albert, who loathed summer holidays, was happier at work; but Flora went with a nursemaid and one or two other servants to Castlerock. Clive and Warren loved the place. The journey begins with a ride in a hansom cab to the railway station. The boys just delight in the train journey that steams its way along the coastline to the backdrop of the nine Glens of Antrim. A high plateau, cut by the deep glens that sweep eastward to the sea, dominates the landscape. They pass gentle bays separated by blunt headlands and exposed moorlands that give way to gentle valleys and wide vistas, that in turn give way to enclosed farmland. Maybe, at Ballymoney Station, they recited the little doggerel much loved by Ulster schoolchildren, referring to actual places in their province:

If you weren't so Ballymena,
And you had some Ballymoney,
You could buy a Ballycastle
To be your Ballyholme.

Castlerock, the Lewis's summer holiday home, was hugely important in Clive's spiritual development. What was the little town like in 1905? Again, our *Belfast and Province of Ulster Directory* of 1905 proves to be invaluable. It tells us that Castlerock is "a pleasant and rapidly-rising watering-place close to the Belfast and Northern Counties Railway Line, advancing in popularity year after year, as shown by the increasing number of visitors who annually patronise it."

> It has also become a favourite resort for Sunday School excursions. In bygone years its visitors were almost entirely drawn from the City of Derry and Limavady Districts, but that has ceased, and it is now inhabited during the Summer Season by holiday-seekers from England and Scotland. Its residents are well aware that this little watering place is without rival in these parts. Though relatively small, it has a decided look of superiority. With the exception of several blocks of large houses, it is made up of detached villas surrounded with tastefully laid out gardens and grounds. There is also a beautiful strand—behind which are the sand-hills, with their tufts of tall wiry looking grass—which stretches along the coast for nearly a mile, to the mouth of the River Bann, where the two piers—one 1,920 feet, and the other 3,680 feet—extend from the sand-hills seaward. There is good bathing accommodation provided, and boxes are erected among the rocks for both classes of bathers. On the Western side of the town on the bold headlands is situated Downhill Castle, the seat of Sir H. Hervey-Bruce, Bart., HML, who was the last sitting Member of Parliament for the Borough of Coleraine.

We learn that there is a golf club and a recreation club with facilities for lawn tennis and cricket. There are two schools, namely Castlerock and Articlave. There is a Post Office, a

Police Barracks, and Refreshment Rooms at the North Counties Railway Station. There are around fifty inhabitants listed, and thirteen local farming families.

Clive Lewis took to the water early, and being immersed in water was a pleasure which he would love for the rest of his life. In fact, being in the water was more pleasurable to him than actually swimming. What effect did the sand, the crabs, the rock pools, the boats, and the ambience of Castlerock have upon him? Probably, they were the seeds of his romantic love of "Northerness." "One of the most important of his feelings was sown during these seaside holidays," writes his friend, George Sayer.[4] Anyone who knows the area would not doubt him. The long skyline, fringed by Downhill and the Mussenden Temple, the distant hills of County Donegal and Innishowen Head, draws the heart and mind like a magnet.

We have pored over the maternal, psychological, and environmental background to little Clive Lewis's childhood; we have traced the emotions, the rhetoric, and the literary leanings of his father; we have looked at the brilliant, logical mind of his mother, and the link of literature between them. All these elements are vital in understanding the genius being moulded in the life of C. S. Lewis; but what about the spiritual element?

C. S. Lewis wrote of three great impressions that touched his childhood that he considered to be absolutely central to what he was about. He records standing by a flowering currant bush one summer's day, when he had a flash of memory. He remembers a morning at his family's first home when his brother brought into the nursery a toy garden in a biscuit tin that he had created for Clive. The garden was made of tiny flowers, twigs, stones, and moss. Suddenly, he was overwhelmed with a sensation. Later, he felt that the nearest thing to it was what Milton called "the enormous bliss" of Eden. It was, Lewis said, a sensation of desire; but it was gone, even before he knew what it was he desired. Passionately, he longed for the longing he had just felt and lost.

He again glimpsed this desire, this sensation, when reading Beatrix Potter's *Squirrel Nutkin*. He called it "the Idea of Autumn."[5] Perhaps it was a glimpse of the impermanence of things; for later he described this present life as being like an inn by the side of the road; and the idea, he said, troubled him.

The third experience of this sensation occurred while reading Longfellow's *Saga of King Olaf*:

I heard a voice that cried,
Balder the beautiful
Is dead, is dead.

He writes of being again uplifted into the whole realm of northern sky. The sensation of desire was beyond description, except that it was "cold, spacious, severe, pale and remote."[6] The description sounds very like an Irish sky at Castlerock after an Irish shower! He described all three experiences by one word: joy.

So it was from a toy garden in a biscuit tin at Dundela Villas, from the pen of the most famous Fell Farmer in England's Lake District, and from a poem about the death of Balder the beautiful that the young C. S. Lewis was touched by intimations of immortality. He didn't hear of it in a sermon; he didn't read of it in a Christian book. The momentary state of joy came from what seemed like something very ordinary, something that led into another world—a presently unknown Eden that was simply beyond words.

Which of us have not had similar moments—moments when we have felt there is something more than the world we live in? We suddenly see something beautiful, and it is so beautiful it makes us ache. Why? Because when it comes, there are within it intimations of something even more beautiful—something unspeakable, even. That there are more beautiful things outside of this world is a truth seriously believed by men and women such as, for example, the Apostle Paul. "I know a man who," he wrote, "fourteen years ago, was seized by Christ and swept into ecstasy to the heights of heaven. I really don't know if this took place in the body or out of it; only God knows. I also know that this man was hijacked into paradise—again, whether in or out of the body, I don't know; God knows. There he heard the unspeakable spoken, but was forbidden to tell what he heard."[7] Explain that!

The truth is that humankind has not so much lost its way as it has lost its address. What we long for, though often we are not aware of it, is for Eden to be restored. The Scriptures assure us that it will be restored:

> The wolf also shall dwell with the lamb, the leopard shall lie down with the young goat, the calf and the young lion and the fatling together; and a little child shall lead them. The cow and the bear shall graze; their young ones shall lie down together; and the lion shall eat straw like the ox. The nursing child shall play by the cobra's hole and the weaned child shall put his hand in the viper's den. They shall not hurt nor destroy in all My Holy Mountain, for the earth shall be full of the knowledge of the Lord as the waters cover the sea. (Isaiah 11: 6-9)

The little seven-year-old boy who, on 21 April 1905, moved with his family into Little Lea on Belfast's Circular Road would one day be used to show millions where to find their lost address. But first he had to find it for himself.

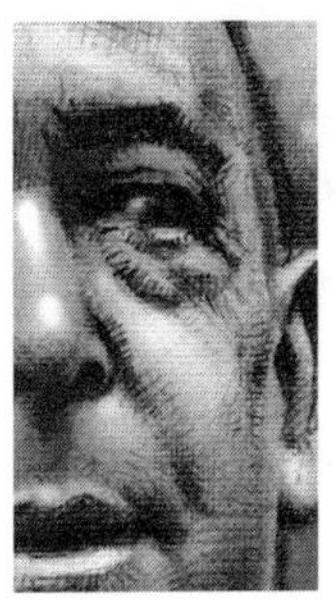

Chapter Two

THE UNBENDING THUMB

What's in a name? A whole lot! Take, for example, the humble potato. It was first cultivated some 7,000 years ago on the wind-swept Andes Mountains in South America, at elevations of up to 15,000 feet. Western man did not come in contact with the potato until as late as 1537, when the Conquistadores tramped through Peru. It was not until about 1570 that the first potato made its way across the Atlantic to the continent of Europe.

As for names given to the potato, they make an interesting study. There are about 3,000 varieties in all. There are, for example, Russets, with some major varieties called Burbank, Centennial, and Morning Gold. In the United States today there are Long Whites, a major variety of which is called White Rose. There are Round Whites, some major varieties of which are called Katahdin, Superior, and Chipeta. There are even Round Reds, with varieties called La Rouge, Red La Soda, and Red Pontiac. In the British Isles there are British Queen, Maris Piper, Jersey Royal, King Edward, and even the Ulster varieties which include Kerr's Pink. Sir Walter Raleigh was the first to introduce the potato to Ireland. In October 1995 it was the first vegetable to be grown in space.

Why do I raise the subject of the potato in the life of C. S. Lewis? It was the nickname that Clive and Warren Lewis gave to their father, Albert. They called him "the Pudaita," or "the Pudaitabird," or just plain "P." The spelling reflects the way Albert pronounced the word "potato" in his Ulster accent. Over many years his boys were to collect his sayings, which they copied into a notebook entitled "Pudaita Pie"! In the Lewis household, Albert was not the only one to get an extra name. One day, the little four-year-old Clive Lewis was being very stubborn. He suddenly refused to answer to his name. "He is Jacksie! He is Jacksie!" he insisted, pointing to himself. What had happened? Clive wanted to be called after a little dog which had lived near his home but had gotten run over in an accident. For the rest of his life, C. S. Lewis became known as "Jacks" to his family and "Jack" to his friends.

Albert's new nickname, though given in affection, was an indication of something that lay very deep in the Irish psyche. Thirty-one years before the Lewises moved into their new home, blight on Ireland's potato crop had led to the Great Irish Famine of 1846 to 1850. It took the lives of as many as one million, through hunger and disease, and profoundly changed the social and cultural structure of Ireland. The Famine spurred new waves of immigration and thereby changed the histories of the United States and Britain. As a result of the Famine, Ireland's population dropped from eight million to five million. The Famine altered agricultural practises that had been going on for centuries; happily, it led to the end of the division of family estates into tiny lots, which were dangerously given over entirely to a potato crop. This little poem remains true to the island of Ireland, North and South, to this day:

The potatoes they grow small over there;
The potatoes they grow small over there.
And they plant them in the fall;
And they eat them skin and all,
Over there.

At the beginning of the twentieth century, in Belfast, the available food was much more varied than it was in the blighted century that had just passed. The Ormeau Bakery was producing its famous fruit loaf and barmbrack. Its baps were part of the very culture of the city—these were cherry buns sprinkled with sugar. They were the inspiration for one of Belfast's best-known ditties:

My Aunt Jane she called me in,
She gave me tea out of her wee tin.
Half a bap with sugar on the top,
And three black lumps out of her wee shop.

Whether Jack and Warren Lewis ever ate the black lumps known as aniseed balls, popular with children at the time, one cannot prove. The city population as a whole certainly had access to fresh fish, "new-laid" eggs, and the ever-popular potato bread, which was in fact griddled bread. Irish hospitality is akin to that of America's Deep South, and its populace knows something of the truth of the rhyme, "Mrs. Foggerty's Christmas Cake":

There were plums and prunes and cherries;
There was citrus and raisins and cinnamon too;

There was nutmeg, cloves, and berries;
And a crust that was nailed on with glue.
There were caraway seeds in abundance,
Such that work up a fine stomach-ache
That could kill a man twice, after eating a slice
Of Mrs. Foggerty's Christmas cake.

Martha, the cook at the Lewises' home, was kept busy feeding the household. Albert's father lived with the family; he was an elderly deaf man, well known for walking around slowly, often humming psalm tunes. The family also employed a gardener, and their maid was Miss Lizzie Endicott from County Down. Jack's memory of childhood always held Lizzie as flawless. She was a lady full of fun, kindness, and the common sense that, if the truth is told, is not so common. Jack called Lizzie a blessing, and indeed she contributed much to his young life, giving him knowledge of country ways. It was Lizzie, and not his mother, who usually did the reading and story telling. It was Lizzie who first told him the fairy story of the three bears and many others. She passed on to him the stories she had heard as a child in County Down, stories of Cuchulain (pronounced KooHoolin), known as the hound of Ulster, one of the most famous Celtic heroes of all time. He was the central figure of the Ulster Cycle, a series of tales revolving around the heroes of the Kingdom of Ulster early in the first century. Cuchulain's story has been described as an old Irish version of the Incredible Hulk: terrifying, possessing superhuman rage, yet when the need arose he could be a gentle, sensitive mortal. He had prodigious strength and remarkable beauty. In the greatest story of the Ulster legends, "The Cattle Raid of Cooley," Cuchulain stood at a ford on the boundary of the Province of Ulster and defended it single-handedly against the armies of the rest of Ireland. The story is told in the oldest vernacular in Western Europe.

Other legends Lizzie told included such heroes as the third-century Finn McCool—warrior, chieftain, poet, and seer—who protected Ireland's coastline from invaders. He is the giant associated in legend with the famous Giant's Causeway, just along the coastline from Castlerock.

Jack was so fired up by these tales that on one occasion he persuaded his brother Warren to help him dig a hole in their front garden at Dundela Villas. Jack and Warren had been looking at a rainbow and decided that in their front garden was the spot where the rainbow had ended. On returning home from his office, their father fell into the hole. When he asked his son for an explanation, Jack told him they were searching for a crock of gold! Understandably, Albert accused him of lying. In fact, Jack was doing anything but lying; one of Lizzie's stories had referred to a crock of gold, and the little boy wanted to find it. Indeed, such stories would one day inspire him to write some legendary tales of his own.

Jack and Warren had a governess, a little Presbyterian lady called Miss Annie Harper. One day, between teaching Jack maths and handwriting, she interposed with a talk that made a very deep impression upon him. He later wrote that the talk was the first thing he could remember that "brought the other world" to his mind "with any sense of reality."[1] So, Lizzie Endicott and Annie Harper can take the credit for introducing Jack to fairytales and to spiritual truths. Combined, they have a lot of glorious writing to answer for!

Jack later stated that his childhood had another blessing, namely his brother, Warren. It seems that during Jack's childhood there was not a lot of mixing with other children, so it was a blessing that the two brothers were also good friends. At Little Lea the brothers enjoyed quite a lot of attics, and in one of them Jack set up his "study." Here he kept pen, ink, writing books, and a paint box; and it was here that he wrote his first stories of Animal-Land, stories containing mice, and rabbits in chain mail who rode out to kill cats. Warren shared Jack's world and greatly admired his brother's ability to write stories and draw pictures. Warren also created a play world of his own called India. A little cistern-room up in the roof of Little Lea actually became the model for the beginning of the adventures in Jack's famous children's book *The Magician's Nephew*.

Jack desperately missed Warren when, at ten years of age, he was sent to board at Wynyard School in Watford, Hertfordshire; but he appreciated his brother all the more when he returned in the school holidays and Jack was able to share with Warren his imaginary Animal-Land. Warren loved drawing trains and steamships, and soon an Animal-Land transport system was introduced, whereby Jack's Animal-Land was linked geographically to Warren's India by steamship routes. No doubt, Warren's ships were inspired by the great shipyard nearby and the moan of ships' horns on Belfast Lough. Jack even wrote a history of Animal-Land, covering centuries of time; Sir Peter Mouse was one of his great characters, as was King Boy, who reigned in the fourteenth century. Up there in the roof of Little Lea in their secret retreat, the Lewis boys had quite a kingdom.

All through history many people have achieved enormously successful lives despite having a disability. Helen Keller, for example, when she was less than two years old contracted an illness that left her unable to see or hear. Family and friends suggested that she be institutionalised because of her "terrorising behaviour," but her parents found a partially blind teacher called Ann Sullivan. After a month of very real struggle, one day outside at the water pump Helen finally grasped the concept of language. Helen Keller graduated from Radcliff College in June 1904, becoming the first deaf-blind person to earn a Bachelor of Arts degree. She went on to become a leading campaigner for civil rights, women's suffrage, and world peace.

We think also of someone like President Roosevelt who in spite of the infirmity of polio became one of the truly great Presidents of the United States. In twenty-first-century Britain, we could think of Stephen Hawking who at the age of twenty-one, discovered that he had Motor Neuron disease. Professor Hawking eventually required a wheelchair to get around and lost his ability to talk, but he has spent his life working on the laws that govern the universe and has developed many scientific theories, particularly regarding black holes and his theory that the universe has no boundary in imaginary time.

As it turned out, Jack and Warren Lewis both had a physical defect that they inherited from their father: they had only one joint in their thumbs. The upper joint, though visible, could not bend. Jack simply couldn't make anything with his hands; using scissors as he tried to cut cardboard drove him to tears many times. For a little boy with such imagination, the frustration must have been enormous. But it led him to his crock of gold; it made him turn instead to writing stories. He maintained that someone could do more with a castle in a story than with any cardboard castle that ever stood on a nursery table. All things that happen to us are not good—that's for sure; but the Bible assures us that they *work together for good to those who love God*.[2] The old Irish proverb is accurate: when God shuts a door, He opens a window.

Jack's father enthusiastically encouraged his writing abilities; but, of course, there were books everywhere at Little Lea. There were books on the landing, books in the cloakroom, books piled up in a bedroom, even books in the cistern attic. All of them were on hand for Jack to read. He plunged into the works of writers including John Milton, Mark Twain, E. Nesbit, Sir Arthur Conan Doyle, Jonathan Swift, and Beatrix Potter. All this between the ages of six and nine!

In the mornings, with Warren away in England, Jack's mother taught him French and Latin. I wonder if he felt about Latin as many other Ulster children do:

Latin is a dead language,
Dead as dead could be;
First it killed the Romans,
And now it's killing me!

Mother and son grew closer and were often to be seen taking afternoon walks together. In the summer of 1907 Flora took her boys on holiday to France to improve their French. They went to a seaside village called Beneval, near Dieppe. On the way home they stopped in London, and Jack revelled in a visit to the Tower of London and London Zoo.

As the year 1908 got going, one of the saddest of all Jack's experiences was beginning to surface. His mother felt very unwell and was soon diagnosed with abdominal cancer. The mother he loved, the pale, blue-eyed mother, who had such a sunny disposition, was now faced with an operation at home.

One night Jack was ill with a headache and toothache and became distressed because his mother did not come to him. There were lots of comings and goings all over the many-roomed house; doors kept opening and shutting. Several doctors were in his mother's room. After what seemed like hours, his father came in tears to Jack's room and conveyed to him the nature of his mother's illness. She had cancer. Jack then set himself to pray for his mother's recovery. He later confessed that he had approached God during that time as if He were a magician, without any sense of love, awe, or fear.

After the operation at Little Lea on 15 February 1908, Flora recovered, and in May she was able to go with Jack to the seaside. Things began to look up; but heartbreakingly Flora was in bed again by June. It was back to fever and delirium and pain-killing morphia. Jack longed to cure his mother; just how deeply was movingly portrayed many years later when he wrote *The Magician's Nephew* in Oxford. In the book Digory Kirk, at the peril of his own life, seeks and finds the Apple of Youth and gives it to his dying mother, who recovers. The sadness of 1908 at Little Lea would never be far away from Jack's mind.

On the night of 21 August, Albert Lewis spoke to his wife of the goodness of God. He recorded her response in one of his notebooks: "What have we done for Him?"[3] She died at 6.30 on the morning of 23 August 1908.

"What have we done for him?" It is a good question in any century. The motto of the City of Belfast is *Pro Tanto Quid Retribuamus*, which may be freely translated, "What return shall we make for so much?" It is said to be based on the words of Psalm 116:12: "What shall I render unto the Lord for all His benefits towards me?" Flora could never have dreamt that her little boy, to whom she had given love, kindness, and guidance, would become one of the greatest writers of children's literature in the world and one of its most gifted Christian apologists. In those first ten years of his life, and particularly in those long, happy summers at Castlerock, Flora Lewis had given Jack one of the greatest gifts any mother could ever give: her time. From that gift came, amongst other things, Jack's awesome sense of Northerness—from which the world got the land of Narnia.

Do not think that I am exaggerating. Kathryn Ann Lindskoog, who knew Jack personally and whose life was changed and deepened through reading his works, tells the story of Jack's last piece of writing for publication. It was an article entitled "We Have No Right to Happiness" for *The Saturday Evening Post* in the United States. It was about sex. Apparently, a friend named Nevill Coghill called and asked Lewis how he happened to be writing for such a popular magazine. Jack explained that the editors thought he was full of paradoxical ideas, so they named a subject and paid him generously. The friend asked Lewis if he was busy inventing some paradoxes. "Not a bit of it," he replied. "What I do is to recall, as well as I can, what my mother used to say on the subject, eke it out with a few similar thoughts of my own, and so produce what would have been strict orthodoxy in about 1900. And this seems to them outrageously paradoxical, *avant-garde* stuff."[4] His eked-out thoughts were, of course, marked with his own genius as a writer, as he argued in a devastating and at times witty fashion against immorality, and in favor of faithfulness within marriage. He warned that if the idea of unrestrained self-gratification took hold, it would sooner or later seep through our lives, and every impulse of every man would be his own law. Then our civilisation would die at its heart and be swept away. Ah, Flora and Jack were to be a formidable intellectual pair across the twentieth century! The mother who nurtured Jack with a cheerful and tranquil affection and undergirded him with intellectual stimulation, by God's grace would achieve more than she could have envisaged.

Jack's great friend David Bleakley told me that Jack had once asked him which was worse: a child's losing his mother at birth, or losing her at ten years of age. There is no doubt that Jack felt it was the latter. No wonder he likened his mother's death to the sinking of *Atlantis*. It would still be some time before Jack discovered for himself that his mother's God was no magician. Awesomely, he would learn that there is no God but God and that He can give us grace to will His will. Jack's unbending thumb would hold a pen through which God would bring incalculable blessing.

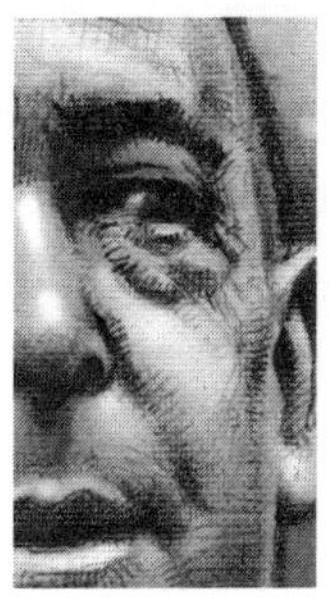

Chapter Three

THE WACKFORD SQUEERS OF WATFORD

Belfast Lough is a large, open sea Lough located on the northeastern coast of the Province of Ulster. It is a curving, thirty-two-kilometer stretch of sheltered water nestling between the hills of County Antrim and County Down. These waters create a channel leading up to one of the busiest ports on the island of Ireland: Belfast Harbour. The mouth of the Lough is defined to the north by the lighthouse at Blackhead and to the south by the town of Groomsport and the Copeland Islands. The inner part of the Lough comprises areas of inter-tidal foreshore, mainly mud-flats, lagoons, and land, areas which are important feeding and roosting sites for significant numbers of wintering waders and wild fowl.

Over winter the area regularly supports over twenty thousand individual waterfowl, including golden eye, red shank, tern, great crested grebe, cormorant, shelduck, black-tailed godwit, curlews, ringed plover, eider, lapwing, and the guillemots at Bangor. While the inner Lough comprises a series of mudflats and lagoons, the outer Lough is composed mainly of rocky shores and some small sandy bays.

The ambience of the area is perhaps best caught in a little anonymous verse entitled *The Blackbird of Belfast Lough*. In a translation by Frank O'Connor, the verse reads thus:

What little throat
Has framed that note?
What gold beak shot
It far away?
A blackbird on
His leafy throne
Tossed it alone
Across the bay.

Sometimes, when I stand by one of those little bays of the outer Lough listening to a blackbird's song or a curlew's call, or walk on the foreshore, I think of Jack Lewis. It is a fact that, apart from his many crossings to and from Belfast Harbour, Jack's travels were for the most part only in his mind. But few minds can have travelled as far, and the Lough played an important emotional role in Jack's life. During his lifetime, it was the exit and entrance point to his homeland, as he frequently boarded the steamship to the English ports of Fleetwood or Liverpool.

An advertisement from the early 1900s for *The Lancashire and Yorkshire and London and North Western Railway* reads as follows:

> Most direct and expeditious route between England and North of Ireland via Fleetwood and Belfast
> The Royal Mail Train Twin Screw Steamships

Duke of Clarence, Duke of Connaught,
Duke of Cornwall, Duke of Lancaster, Duke of York.

The advertisement informs the reader that sailings took place every evening with "Sundays and Casualties excepted." Fares were Saloon 12s6d. Steerage 5s…children above three and under twelve years of age were half fare.

According to the Fleetwood Boat advertisement, Jack was certainly still a child when he began to prepare for one of their sailings. He put on a broad, stiff, white collar called an Eton collar; a pair of loose-fitting breeches, known as knickerbockers, buttoned tightly just below the knee; and a thick, prickly suit of some heavy serge-type material. He wore stiff, heavy, new boots. Finally, he put on a bowler hat and set off with his father and brother in a four-wheeled carriage across the cobbled streets of Belfast for a very new chapter in his already eventful life.

The widowed Albert Lewis did not find it easy to say goodbye to his two boys. In the year that he had lost his wife, he also lost his brother and his father, who lived with them at Little Lea. Albert boarded the ship and paced the deck for some time, and then, filled with deep emotion, he took leave of his sons. They were embarrassed and self-conscious at this display of feeling. Somewhat relieved to leave him, they turned to explore the ship as she slipped her moorings and sailed down Belfast Lough into what turned out to be a rough crossing. Warren was seasick, but Jack turned out to be a good sailor.

Jack's first impressions of England were not good. The following morning around six o'clock the boys boarded a train alongside the steamer at Fleetwood for London Euston. As the train steamed across Lancashire, Jack reacted with a feeling of hatred. Everything looked different from what he was accustomed to. Jack was always to be an Ulsterman abroad. He carried a deep sense of the Holywood and Castlereagh Hills, of Scrabo Hill and Strangford Lough, and of the small fields and stone walls of the County Down countryside. The flat landscape of Lancashire that he saw from the train did not appeal to him, and the strange accents all around him jarred. The sea was gone; even the haystacks were the wrong shape. In time he was to view England in a much better light, but first time round he hated the sight of the place! The feeling was no doubt reciprocated, as expressed in the words of this ditty:

Oh Patsy, you're a villain;
Patsy, you're a rogue.
There's nothing of you Irish
Except your name and your brogue.

Jack's immediate misery was to be further compounded. Of all the boarding schools in England, Albert Lewis could not possibly have picked a worse one. And why did he choose a boarding school at all? George Sayer has explained: "Albert's main motive was social, the desire for his sons to attain and preserve the status of gentlemen, to sound and look right, to talk without an accent, to wear the right sort of clothes, and to have good manners (that is, manners acceptable to older men of the same class)."[1] When consulted, Albert's Headmaster, W. T. Kirkpatrick, advised that Jack and Warren be sent to a good prep school in England, in the hope of a scholarship and entrance to an English public school. He recommended a school at Rhyl in North Wales, but Albert chose Wynyard School in Watford. It turned out to be a nightmare, a disaster. Jack called it a concentration camp and nicknamed it Belsen.

When one reads Jack's description of his experiences at Wynyard School, one cannot but think of Dotheboys Hall School in Charles Dickens' *Nicholas Nickleby*. Long before he became a writer, Dickens had heard of the hideous treatment of unwanted children in certain schools in Yorkshire, and he researched his target for satire by visiting Yorkshire and interviewing people there. These included the one-eyed headmaster, whose fictional reincarnation was the cruel and ignorant Headmaster of Dotheboys Hall: the horrendous Wackford Squeers. Dickens' descriptions of the school and of what went on there are unquestionably amongst the most vivid and memorable of all his writings. The descriptions of the torture inflicted on the mentally retarded Smike are some of fiction's most powerful satire. The exploited children of *Nicholas Nickleby* are middle-class children. The book is a powerful attack on cruelty, and the scenes at Dotheboys Hall are amongst Dickens' most popular dramatic readings. One can imagine Dickens stirring an audience with the scene in which Nicholas is driven to distraction by Wackford Squeers' cruelty. Squeers is about to publicly punish Smike for running away from the school:

> "Each boy keep his place," said Squeers, administering his favourite blow to the desk, and regarding with gloomy satisfaction the universal start which it never failed to occasion. He had his gaze fastened on the luckless Smike, as he enquired, according to custom in such cases, whether he had anything to say for himself.
>
> "Nothing, I suppose?" says Squeers, with a diabolical grin. Smike glanced round, and his eye rested for an instant on Nicholas as if he expected him to intercede; but his look was riveted on his desk.

> "Have you anything to say?" demanded Squeers again: giving his right arm two or three flourishes to try its power and suppleness. "Stand a little out of the way, Mrs. Squeers, my dear; I've hardly got room enough."
>
> Mrs. Squeers, being out of breath with her exertions, complied. Squeers caught the boy firmly in his grip; one desperate cut had fallen on his body—he was wincing from the lash and uttering a scream of pain—it was raised again, and again about to fall—when Nicholas Nickleby, suddenly standing up, cried "Stop!" in a voice that made the rafters ring.
>
> "Who cried stop?" said Squeers, turning savagely round.
>
> "I," said Nicholas, stepping forward. "This must not go on."[2]

There follows Dickens' description of how Nicholas felled the ugly tyrant Squeers and left the miserable place to its own fate, taking Smike with him.

Such was the fiction of Dickens; but now we turn to the extraordinary reality for Jack Lewis. For "Wackford Squeers," read "the Reverend Robert Capron," an Anglican clergyman. A physically strong man, he could lift a boy of twelve from the floor by the back of his collar and, holding him at arm's length, flog the calves of his legs. He was, in fact, a bearded, unkempt tyrant. A brain specialist had actually examined the Reverend Capron and found him to be mad.

In the mornings, Oldie, as the boys called him, would enter that single schoolroom in his yellow-bricked house, pick on a boy, and tell him that, in the afternoon, if he was not too tired, he would give him a good beating. Oldie would even make a child bend down at the end of the room, run the length of the room, receive a stroke of the cane, then go back and do the same thing for the next stroke and for all the following strokes. Such caning was not necessarily for bad behaviour, but for, say, a mistake in geometry. If a pupil became confused, Oldie would flog the desk shouting, "Think. Think. Think." Then, before he would do to the boy what he had done to the desk, he would say, "Come out, come out, come out."

When Jack arrived at the school there were eight or nine boarders and around the same number of dayboys. There was only one bathroom for all of them and one bath allowed per week. Organised games had been abandoned at the school shortly after Jack's arrival, rounders being played on a flinty playground. The outside toilets were in an open-fronted, corrugated iron shed. There was only one dormitory, and it had no curtains. Jack used to lie and watch the full moon and the night sky. The teaching in the school was by rote, a method which he found intellectually stupefying.

In between the recitation of lessons, Oldie demanded that his class do sums on slates. At the end of the morning he would ask each boy how many sums he had done. Since supervision was slack, Warren discovered he could do the same five sums every day and not get caught. He did this for years; a more tedious exercise would be hard to imagine.

Oldie's wife, a timid little woman, did not seek to venture any original remark. Discretion was for her the better part of valour. As for Oldie's three daughters, they could have been called "Yes, Papa," "No, Papa," and "Three bags full, Papa." They were always dressed in black, and shabby black at that. Oldie's son, nicknamed Wee-We, also "taught" at the school; and there was one usher, or assistant teacher, who, understandably, rotated frequently. One of them lasted only a week.

How could there be any blessings in such a place of misery? Where could the proverbial silver lining be in such a dark cloud? Jack Lewis later spoke of how the cruelty they experienced at Wynyard School brought all the boys together. They found comfort in their own company, for there was none other. They became sociable. They might not have had organised games, but they did have the freedom to go for walks on half-holidays. They bought sweets in village shops, spent time on the canal bank, and sat on the brow of a railway cutting, waiting for trains to come out of the mouth of the tunnel. Why are we not surprised when we learn that Jack had a discussion with his fellow pupils on whether the future was like an unseen line, or like a line not yet drawn?

The God who knows the future was at work in this child's life. Attending St. John's Anglican Church in Watford, Jack heard Christian truth taught by men who believed it. He began to read the Bible and to pray. He listened to his conscience. It is worth asking how the one who would inspire millions of children could be inspired in such a horrible school. How could the one who would bring messages of hope to a nation threatened, not by a cruel clergyman, but by a tyrant called Hitler, find hope for himself?

The touching thing is that, years later, when reflecting on his experience at Wynyard, Jack maintained that it was all a good preparation for the Christian life, because it taught him to live by hope! This is a profound and helpful point, because hope is not just a nice option; it is essential to our survival. It lifts our spirits, it keeps us going, it saves us from panicking, and it helps us to persevere through the immediate circumstances. Hope fuels our recovery from life's disasters. Without hope, marriages would go dry, students would never finish their courses, addicts would be forever enslaved in their habits, and artists, entrepreneurs, and inventors would all lose their creativity. Hope forces us to wait for better things. At Wynyard School, the little boy Jack lived in hope.

Lewis also said that at that time he learned to live, in a sense, by faith. Faith, of course, is being sure of what we hope for, and certain of what we do not see. At the beginning of a term, he considered home and the holidays to be as hard to realise as Heaven itself; yet what was so hard to realise always came. Lewis claimed that the memories of those dreadful times made the life of faith easier.

In 1910 Oldie retired to become the vicar of a church, where he began to flog the choirboys for no apparent reason. When the churchwardens tried to stop him, he flogged them as well. He resigned from that church after just one year. He was eventually put under restraint and declared insane. He died on the eighteenth of November in 1911.

Jack learned that the hard times might look like an impossible situation, but they were not the end. He learned that, by exercising faith and hope, there was more to what immediately met his eye. As the children in *The Lion, the Witch and the Wardrobe* passed from war-torn Britain into Narnia, so he would pass into greater things. When he would have his adult heart broken by overwhelming sorrow, and eventually face illness and death, he, too, would experience the truth, as stated by Aslan in *The Last Battle*, of a place where "the term is over: the holidays have begun. The dream is ended: this is the morning."[3]

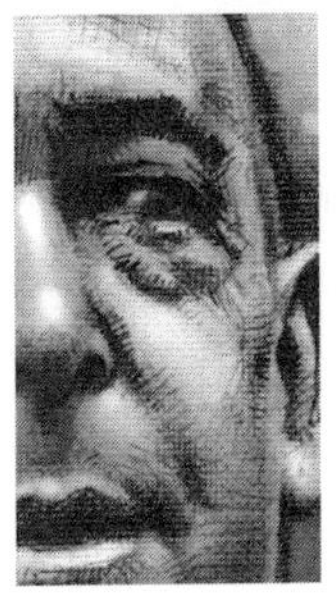

Chapter Four

THE MOST BEAUTIFUL WOMAN HE EVER SAW

It was glorious! Jack and Warren Lewis were cycling in the beautiful County Down countryside, with "the world as their oyster" for two whole months. The roads and lanes they followed were narrow; their width had been untouched for centuries. The hedges were high, and the land was planted with crops and fruit trees. The fields were lavishly dotted with herds of sheep and dairy cattle that in time would create the basis of one of the strongest agricultural industries in Europe.

All across North and East Down, the countryside through which they cycled was filled with little huddles of heavily whitewashed farm buildings. The boys panted heavily up one side, and breathed easily down the other side of the little drumlins.

The name *drumlin* is Irish. It is the name given to a mound of land characteristic of areas formerly covered by glaciers. Drumlins are shaped like the bowl of a teaspoon turned upside down, with the highest part near one end. Hundreds of drumlins enhanced the landscape of County Down, creating the pleasant rolling farmland that was so greatly loved by Jack and Warren.

What had happened in the lives of these two boys? For a start, the Reverend Robert Capron had stopped beating the boys at Wynyard. It was not because he had changed, of course. He no longer had any boys to beat, for the school had had to close in 1910 for lack of pupils. Jack had written to his father, asking to leave the school, and Albert sent his sister-in-law to investigate. She faced Capron, and as a result of the showdown things did improve at Wynyard School for a time. Fortunately, Capron had never beaten Jack. In September 1909 Warren had gone on to Malvern School, leaving Jack to endure Wynyard for two more terms. For the next fifty years, he was to resent and feel anger towards Oldie. Who could blame him? In fact, Jack was not able to forgive Oldie until the last year of his life. That he survived Wynyard School to become the man he was is a triumph of hope over circumstances.

Hope had been satisfied with the end-of-term holidays; but now it was more deeply satisfied with the end of Wynyard. For Jack and Warren, the holidays had been the main goal of their existence so far. Not only did they cycle across the beautiful County Down countryside, but also they wrote, drew, played, talked, and read books in that home of books. It must have been bliss to be home. The boys were inseparable, and any interruption—be it another child, or the social convention of having to go to adult evening parties that included dancing—was viewed as sheer persecution.

Quite naturally, from all this reading, Jack's speech was peppered with formidable words. To his great discomfort, he found that adults would lead him on in conversation just to laugh at him. To circumvent the problem, at every party he went to he affected a style of conversation that offered nothing that would stimulate or challenge. Under a guise of imitating adult conversation, laced with joking and false enthusiasm, he deliberately hid what he thought and felt. He became a consummate actor, and it was with great relief that he joined Warren for the cab ride home—the best part of the night, as far as he was concerned.

In terms of communication, the gap between teenagers and adults seems to have been every bit as wide in Edwardian days as it is now in the twenty-first century. Jack later maintained that one family bridged that gap in a way that made a deep and lasting impression upon him. That was the Ewart family. Sir William Ewart was a Belfast merchant and linen manufacturer. In 1864 he was one of the deputies from Belfast involved in the arrangements for a treaty of commerce with France. He was the Member of Parliament for Belfast East, Justice of the Peace for the Counties of Antrim, Down, and the Borough of Belfast, and Lord Mayor of Belfast from 1859 to 1860. A baronetcy was conferred on him in 1887. He and his wife, Isabella, had seven sons, who were all in their father's business. The eldest, Sir William Quartus Ewart, lived at the family seat, Glenmachan House. In Jack's childhood days the house was in a wooded glen. Sir William was married to Flora Lewis's cousin, Lady Mary Ewart. Flora and Lady Mary were the very best of friends. There was an open invitation for Jack and Warren to lunch at Glenmachan House, and later Jack was to write a very warm and moving tribute to the family's kindness.

It was under Lady Mary's kindly eye and by her lilting, memorable, Southern Irish accent that the Lewis boys were taught to be polite, courteous, and well mannered. They needed such teaching, but it was no dictatorial regime that reigned at Glenmachan House; people further removed from the behaviour of the Wackford Squeers of Watford could not have been found. The boys enjoyed wise-headed and warm-hearted benevolence there; yet a high standard of manners was set and kept at Glenmachan House.

In the twenty-first century the pendulum of manners has swung widely in the opposite direction. When the two top swearwords in Britain are "God" and "Christ," we are in a serious spiritual situation. People say they don't mean anything by such language, of course. Yet the Bible states that we should *not take the name of the Lord in vain*. This means that we must not use the name of the Lord in our conversation without ascribing profitable meaning to it.

There has been strong reaction against some Edwardian etiquette as being too stiff and formal. No doubt such a reaction is healthy, but Jack Lewis came to appreciate that not all Edwardian etiquette was irrelevant. He had a formidable etiquette to follow. Imagine applying what was expected of an Edwardian gentleman to twenty-first-century living.

The Edwardian gentleman was always to be dressed neatly, and his clothing must never be loud or ostentatious. His nails must be scrupulously clean and his hair neatly combed and free from dirt or oil. He must carry himself erectly, but not stiffly. His spine must be straight, his shoulders back. He must always aspire to calm confidence rather than to loftiness. He must never put his hands in his pockets. His hands should hang comfortably at his sides or be clasped behind him. A gentleman must never smoke in the presence of a lady, or in the street, or in church. Smoking was for the smoking room or the presence of other smokers. A gentleman was always expected to ask permission before lighting a cigarette. And a gentleman was never, ever, to spit.

When in the company of a lady, an Edwardian gentleman was expected to see to her every need and want. He must pull out a chair for her, rise when she rose, hold open doors for her, assist her out of a carriage, and if she should drop her handkerchief or other such item he must pick it up. A gentleman was expected to precede a lady into a room in order to provide a chair for her, and he was expected not to sit until she was seated. As the era proceeded, a gentleman was expected to assist a lady into a motorcar. A gentleman was expected never to make anyone feel awkward. Upon entering a room, a gentleman was expected to greet everyone pleasantly and to introduce himself to those he did not know.

As for table manners, a very clear etiquette was to be observed. While waiting to be served, a gentleman was never to play with his knife and fork. He was not to hold them vertically at the sides of his plate. When his meal was finished he was never to cross his knife and fork, and he was always to use them noiselessly. Under no circumstances was he to put his knife into his mouth; his knife must be used only for cutting meat and hard substances. He must never appear greedy, and he must always take small bites. He must never speak with his mouth full. If his hands were unoccupied at the table, he must keep them under the table, neatly folded in his lap. If he had to rise from the table he must ask his host or hostess if he might be excused. If he were to find a hair or a fly or any unpleasant object in his food, he was to remove it subtly and without remark. He must never use his knife, fork, spoon, or finger to serve himself. If no serving utensil was provided, he was to take his cue from his host or hostess. As a dinner guest, he must always keep other people's pleasure in mind. He must never take medications at the table. A golden rule was that he must never take more than he could finish. He must not allow his silverware to touch the table after he had picked it up. He must not smack his lips. He must never slurp his soup, and he was always expected to spoon his soup away from him, starting from the outside of the bowl. Were these requirements too much? No doubt they were. But good manners are easily carried through life. Later Jack maintained that whatever he knew of the ability to act appropriately and with courtesy in social situations, he had learned at Glenmachan House.

Jack thought the world of the grey-bearded Sir William. He was a kindly, humble, and gracious Edwardian gentleman. To Jack, the gentle, coaxing hand and voice of Sir William's wife, Lady Mary Ewart, meant a great deal. Could it be that the frequent passivity of an older generation towards the young has led to the banality of much in current Western culture?

Sir William's three daughters—Hope, Kels, and Gundreda—used to take the Lewis boys out in their donkey trap pulled by an obstinate donkey called Grisella. (Ah! When Gundreda urged Grisella to move on, it must have been something else! Don't you think somebody should write a poem about it?) The Ewart family took the boys with them on many walks, car trips, picnics, and visits to the theatre. Glenmachan House was a home-from-home, and in many ways a calmer home than Little Lea.

Jack maintained that Gundreda Ewart was the most beautiful woman he ever saw. This belief had nothing to do with having a boyish crush for her. He asserted that even a child could see her beauty. To him, her every movement, her colour, her voice, her laughter were absolutely perfect.

Gundreda not only possessed beauty; she also possessed a fascinating name, to say the least. We know that Jack's mother was a Warren; her ancestry can be traced to an Anglo-Norman whose family had been planted in Ireland in the reign of Henry II. The now dissolved C. S. Lewis Centenary Group, who produced the *C. S. Lewis News,* have told us that this Anglo-Norman was William de Warrenne, one of the greatest of William the Conqueror's barons. To De Warrenne was given in marriage Gundreda, the Conqueror's reputedly illegitimate daughter. Through Gundreda, wife of William de Warrenne, C. S. Lewis was descended from William the Conqueror and Charlemagne! The Centenary Group also pointed out that, through this aristocratic connection to the Warrennes, C. S. Lewis "was descended from the Plantagenet Kings of England, Kings of France, Scots, and Princes of Wales."[2] The genealogy of Jack's beautiful cousin Gundreda certainly goes back a very long way.

In July 1910 Jack left Wynyard and the rule of Oldie, and for half a term he attended a school only one mile from his home in Belfast, called Campbell College. For Jack, it was actually the very first time he could say the little Belfast ditty:

Jack Lewis is my name;
Ireland is my nation.
Belfast is my dwelling place;
And school's my occupation.

Campbell College was founded through the benevolence of a wealthy linen merchant called Henry James Campbell; it has since become a famous school in Northern Ireland. Set in the beautiful and tranquil hundred-acre Campbell Estate, today the school provides a balanced and rounded education for 680 boys, and takes around 60 boarders. It is Northern Ireland's equivalent to an English public school; its preparatory school, Cabin Hill, stands in the same grounds. Why on earth did Albert Lewis not send his boys to Campbell College in the first place? It is a question that will always be asked.

Jack was a boarder at Campbell but was allowed to go home on Sundays. The present school leadership states that they believe "boarding helps develop confidence, community spirit, independence, social skills, cultural awareness, and respect for others." The school emphasises that one of its major strengths is its "House System." Each House consists of 50 boys, with the House Master and House Tutors responsible for overseeing the welfare of the boys in their charge in all aspects of their school life. Inter-House competitions in sporting and cultural events are a vital part of the school's life. Today's sporting activities include archery, athletics, badminton, basketball, cricket, cross country, golf, hill-walking, hockey, mountaineering, orienteering, rugby, shooting, soccer, squash, swimming, tennis, and volleyball. There is an orchestra and a jazz band, and the school has a strong choral tradition. The school choir, comprising both staff and boys, leads the morning assembly and performs at special occasions.

In Jack's day, things were very different in many ways. The House system was present, but it was not as strong, and games were not compulsory. Prefects held no prominence.

Today, the Common Rooms at Campbell have satellite TV and DVD players. Access to the Internet is available for e-mail and research purposes. All pupils after year ten have accommodation on an individual-room basis; but in Jack's time only senior boys had a separate study. Two of his overriding memories were the lack of privacy and the noisy Common Rooms.

When reading the description of Lewis's memories of Campbell College, one is reminded of the classic Alexander Sokurov film *The Russian Ark*. It portrays a large crowd of people flowing like a tide down a staircase after a ball, then flowing down a corridor—thinning here, fanning out there, chatting, calling to each other, gossiping, and passing on news. Suddenly, there is an open doorway through which water can be seen stretching away to the horizon. The water is said to represent eternity. Jack described out-of-school hours at Campbell College as either moving away from, or going with, a tide of boys. The description sounds much like the movement of the people in *The Russian Ark*. Jack also described his experience at school as living in a railway station. His metaphor will resonate with many as a childhood memory of school crowds. Eternity still flows beyond the school door; but for the pupil, life is dominated by the here and now. For Jack, the here-and-now meant watching school fights with the ever-prurient crowds. There were "seconds," even, at these boxing matches, attendants who assisted each combatant. Jack reckoned that there was also betting going on. He surmised that fists and wit could win any pupil his place in the life of the school! For Jack, though, any bullying at Campbell amounted to once being shoved down a hatch into a coal cellar. He found himself in the company of another small boy, as part of a game being played by roving gangs of fellow pupils.

Jack must have found Campbell College a Shangri-La in comparison to Wynyard. In the place of Oldie, he found Octie. Octie was the nickname the boys had for Lewis Alden, the Senior English Master at Campbell from 1898 until 1930. As far as Jack was concerned, the most important event to happen to him at Campbell College was to hear Octie read Matthew Arnold's *Sohrab and Rustum*. With his deep, resonant voice, Octie obviously sparked something in Jack's imagination as he read Arnold's masterpiece of heroic, even epic poetry. By the shores of Belfast Lough, in Octie's Form Room, from the very first lines Jack was entranced:

And the first grey of morning fill'd the east,
And the fog rose out of the Oxus stream.
But all the Tartar camp along the stream
Was hush'd, and still the men were plunged in sleep;
Sohrab alone, he slept not; all night long
He had lain wakeful, tossing on his bed;
But when the grey dawn stole into his tent,
He rose, and clad himself, and girt his sword,
And took his horseman's cloak, and left his tent,
And went abroad into the cold wet fog,
Through the dim camp to Peran-Wisa's tent.[3]

The reversal and rhetoric in Arnold's epic story of Sohrab the Tartar and Rustum the Persian—the son and father's edging closer to their fatal combat, in which the father unknowingly kills his son—fired Jack's imagination. As the final lines fell on his ear, telling of the majestic Oxus River floating on, Jack felt that he was gazing at things in a very far country:

Out of the mist and hum of that low land
Into the frosty starlight…
The long'd-for dash of waves is heard, and wide
His luminous home of waters opens, bright
And tranquil, from whose floor the new-bathed stars
Emerge, and shine upon the Aral Sea.

Jack entered into European poetry as never before. It seemed to depict something he longed for, but which was, for now, unattainable. He was only a twelve-year-old boy. He could not have known that he, like Matthew Arnold before him, would begin to have serious doubts about the veracity of the Christian faith. Matthew, son of Thomas Arnold, the famous headmaster of Rugby School and himself a pioneer of state education, found that his doubts brought him great anxiety, as he tried very hard to reconcile "traditional religion" with the conclusions of the new "higher criticism." In his poem *Stanzas from the Grande Chartreuse*, he wrote of "wandering between two worlds, one dead, the other powerless to be born."[4]

In June 1851, Arnold married Frances Lucy Whiteman, daughter of Sir William Whiteman, a judge of the Queen's Bench. At Dover on his honeymoon, Arnold heard the waves raking across the shingle outside his hotel bedroom. And in his poem "Dover Beach" he wrote:

The sea of faith
Was once too at the full and round Earth's shore
Lay like the folds of a bright girdle furl'd:
But now I only hear
Its melancholy long withdrawing roar,
Retreating to the breath
Of the night wind down the vast edges drear
And naked shingles of the world....[5]

Matthew Arnold's journey led to agnosticism; Jack Lewis's led to atheism. Arnold was part of the great ebb of faith throughout Europe, beginning (as mentioned in the preface) particularly with the Deism of the eighteenth-century Scottish aristocrat David Hume. The loss of faith came down through the writings and beliefs of people like Thomas Carlyle, Marx and Engels, the gifted novelist George Eliot, Charles Darwin, Tennyson, Thomas Hardy, John Ruskin, and George Bernard Shaw. This loss of faith among writers, artists, and intellectuals in Western civilisation has had a seismic effect upon our culture.

The twelve-year-old boy was not to know that one day he would be seriously considered for the position of Professor of Poetry at Oxford University, a position which Arnold held for two successive terms of five years. Nor was the boy to know that one day Sir Anthony Hopkins would unveil one of his poems, engraved on a plaque in Oxford itself. Enchanted by the poetry of Arnold at Campbell College, Jack Lewis was not to know that the living God would use him to help turn back the tide of faith once again.

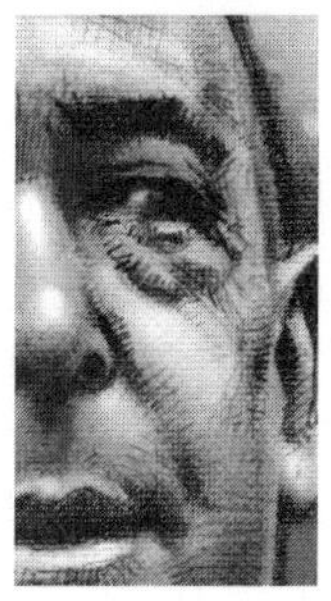

Chapter Five

A CARELESS TONGUE

Autumn had lowered her flag in Ulster, and many of her bright colours were now almost out of sight. On the Circular Road in Belfast, bare boughs were standing gaunt against the November sky. The bracken on the surrounding hills was still yellow; the heather in sheltering nooks still retained a faint blush of pale purple; and the deep crimson leaves of the bramble were visible in the hedgerows. The pretty red and green moss-balls upon the wild-rose brier, known as robin's pincushions, were flourishing. The mosses and lichens on the banks and hillsides were having their springtime; but all around winter was setting in.

The Saxons aply named November "wind month." When its gales return, pines are bent, bracken is ruffled, lake and sea are lashed, and acorns fall heavily in the woods. As Christmas approached in Ireland, the holly bushes of Ulster were beating their polished leaves together.

Early in November 1910, another kind of gale was blowing across the life of young Jack Lewis. He was brought home to Little Lea with a bad cough. The weak-chested Jack was ill and had to be kept at home for the rest of the term—not that he minded! There followed six weeks of solitude into which he entered with great pleasure. Leaving the noise of Campbell College behind, he felt his solitude to be like a refreshing bath. He was never to like crowds. When his father was out at work, Jack wrote, read, and drew to his heart's content; and he fell in love with fairytales. He particularly liked the dwarfs of his fairytales; and one day he wondered if he hadn't seen one darting into the shrubbery!

Jack slept in his father's room at night, and the two got on fine—at this point probably better than they ever would again. Lewis later claimed that, for reasons he did not quite know, his father had become dissatisfied with Campbell College. Not long after Albert's hand influenced Jack's life once more, but more wisely this time. Albert decided to send his weak-chested son to the spa town of Malvern, where Warren was at Malvern School. Jack was sent to its Preparatory School, Cherbourg, which stood on a hill just above Warren's school.

The countryside surrounding Malvern is steeped in outstanding beauty. The College, founded in 1865, is situated in spacious grounds below the Worcestershire Beacon. In the local parish church of St. Wulfstan lies the grave of the great English musician Sir Edward Elgar. Last year, the *Enigma* Fountain was unveiled there in his memory by HRH The Duke of York. The pure water from the Malvern hills, a favourite of the present Queen, was first bottled about 1622, but was appreciated well before that and even long before Queen Elizabeth I granted the Holy Well to the Lord of the Manor. Dr. John Wall, a Worcester physician, first analysed the famous Malvern Water in 1756.

Following the publishing of his book *Experiments & Observations on the Malvern Waters,* Dr. Wall concluded in a famous quotation, "The Malvern water is famous for containing just nothing at all." Malvern became known as a curative centre in 1757 after Dr Wall published his findings. The original well was in an orchard.

In Jack's time, the water of Malvern was already being bottled by Schweppes and was selling all over the country. Nowadays, twelve million litres are bottled and sold annually. The source, now known as Prime Well Spring, flows at an average of approximately sixty litres per minute and has never been known to dry up.

The area is also blessed with an almost alpine dryness; and it would appear that Albert hoped this climate would bring ease to Jack's weak chest. So, in January 1911, Jack moved out of Ulster once more, leaving behind its frequent rainy days. Now entering his teenage years, Jack acquired a much healthier view of England. Although Jack certainly did not think that the hills around him were more beautiful than those of Ireland—and said so when writing home—he did delight in them!

A thirteen-year-old boy who has lost his mother is in great need of somebody to mother him. That mothering he so needed was provided by Cherbourg's gifted matron, Miss Cowie. She showed great kindness to Jack and the other boys, and Jack had a deep and tender affection for her. Jack later hinted that she had had no guide on her spiritual journey to point her to the Saviour of the World. She had turned to consider the teaching of theosophy. In 1875, Mrs. Helena Petrovna Blavatsky, and Col. Henry Steel Olcott founded the Theosophical Society in New York. The society attempted to derive an ethical core from ancient wisdom and from insights into the theory of evolution. Ireland's greatest twentieth-century poet, W. B. Yeats, visited Mrs. Blavatsky and joined the Esoteric Section of the Theosophical Society. He became obsessed with the exploration of mystical phenomena. His biographers, Micheál MacLiammóir and Eavan Boland, said, "this [involvement with theosophy] might be said to have influenced well-nigh every subsequent action of his life. Certainly it became the leading force in his writing, and although his days and nights teemed with a hundred other interests, the quest for the unknown was to remain the changeless background."[1] All of this interest in the unknown led Yeats into the occult, and Jack was later to be influenced by his writing.

His friend, Katherine Tynan, had taken Yeats to his very first séance. "The experience was unnerving for them both," write MacLiammóir and Boland.

> After some chilling preliminaries, swiftly followed by a few alarming words (accompanied by actions) from the medium, Miss Tynan left the table and sank to her knees in prayer in a corner, while Yeats, who had been compelled by some unseen force to bang his neighbour's knuckles on the table, then proceeded to break the table. After that, he felt he was going into a trance, then decided that he was not; and finally, unable to remember a prayer, started to recite the opening of *Paradise Lost*. He then began to sense the presence of something "very evil" in the room.[2]

Did such a journey eventually lead to a lack of real hope? Hopelessness is reflected in the epitaph that he requested for his gravestone in Sligo's Drumcliff Churchyard. The final three lines from his last poem read thus:

Cast a cold Eye
On Life, on Death.
Horseman, pass by!

Mixed with her interest in theosophy, Miss Cowie also explored Rosicrucian thinking. A Rosicrucian was a member of a secretive society devoted to the study of metaphysical, mystical, and alchemical lore. Miss Cowie was also into spiritualism—a system of belief, or religious practise, based on supposed communication with the spirits of the dead, especially through mediums.

In the midst of her duties as matron, Miss Cowie shared her current thinking with Jack, not realising as he put it, that it was as if she was actually carrying a candle into a room full of gunpowder. And Jack was ignited. Were there other worlds that his Christian belief knew nothing about? Was this visible world only a cover for other realms? He rightly came to see his curiosity as a "spiritual lust"; it blinded him to other things. The one whom Jack Lewis later called the Enemy was prowling about and seeking to devour him.

Miss Cowie did not set out to destroy Jack's faith. She had no idea that the more she talked of her spiritual journey, the more she was undermining what Jack believed. Hers was an undefined world, far removed from the mighty framework of the Holy Scriptures with its *Thou shalt nots,* those clear boundaries set up by God to protect heart, mind, soul, and home, as well as family, public, national, and international life. Soon, Jack was altering the strong commitment of "I believe" to the vague, speculative "one does feel." But he felt relieved. "From the tyrannous noon of revelation," he wrote, "I passed into the cool evening of Higher Thought, where there was nothing to be obeyed, and nothing to be believed, except what was either comforting or exciting. I do not mean that Miss Cowie did this: better say the Enemy did this in me, taking occasion from the things she innocently said."[3]

At this point in this biography it is worth pondering a little statement from a publication called *The Biblical Treasury*:

> Suppose my watch was not working well. Would it do any good for me to travel to the town clock, and reset the hands of my watch to match those with the city clock? You know this would do no good, for the hands of my watch would soon be as far wrong as ever. I must send my watch to the watchmaker that he may put its heart right, and then the hands will go right too. So it is with ourselves and our children. We must first get our hearts right, and then our hands will go right, and our feet, and all else.[4]

Sadly, through a careless tongue, the Enemy was subtly wooing Jack's young heart away from his Maker. The Enemy was even fouling up Jack's prayer life; Jack began to have a sense in his conscience that he was not thinking enough about what he was actually saying in his prayers. He started a process of "realisation" which drove him to deep anxiety. Had he continued with it, he reckoned the process would have driven him to insanity. He had no real concept of a Heavenly Father who loved him and who was willing through Christ to accept him just as he was. Prayer was designed to give access to the heart of God, so that we may obtain help in time of need; but the Enemy had turned it into a guilt-inducing exercise. Jack's view of prayer had become far removed from that of his fellow Ulsterman, Joseph Scriven:

Oh what peace we often forfeit;
Oh what needless pain we bear;
All because we do not carry
Everything to God in prayer.

Subconsciously, Jack's struggle with prayer was now being used by the Enemy to make him want to move away from the Christian faith. He restlessly struggled through many long nights. Intellectually, he became pessimistic.

One day in 1949 at the Edwards Air Force Base in the United States, an engineer working on an Air Force project found that a transducer had been wrongly wired. Annoyed with the technician responsible, the engineer said, "If there is any way to do it wrong, he'll find it." The contractor's project manager kept a list of laws, and now added a new one that he called Murphy's Law.[6] It stated, "anything that can go wrong will go wrong." Jack's pessimism went much further than Murphy's Law: he began to expect and believe that *everything* would do what he did not want it to do. Pondering Jack's writing about the pessimism he had as a fourteen-year-old boy, one perceives that the behaviour of Oldie and the death of his mother had caused deep emotional wounds. The grey fog of depression can sweep into the life of a teenager every bit as much as it can sweep into that of an adult.

The philosophy of Miss Cowie certainly did not lift Jack's pessimism. There was no lasting joy or peace on that road; there never has been, and there never will be. "There shall not be found among you anyone who makes his son or daughter pass through the fire," said God to Moses, "or one who practises witchcraft, or a soothsayer, or one who interprets omens, or a Sorcerer, or one who conjures spells or a medium, or a spiritist, or one who calls up the dead; for all who do these things are an abomination to the Lord" (Deuteronomy 18:10-12).

Is it not worth asking ourselves what we can do to help our teenagers? Sadly, the suicide rate is rising among them, especially in Western society. In the north and west of Jack's home city at the time of writing this biography, the rate is almost sixty percent higher than it is anywhere else in the United Kingdom. Many adults are unhappy because the untreated depression from their own teenage years has persisted. It is therefore vital to reach out to teenagers with an encouraging word or kind action. It is important to encourage what gifts they have and to help them reach their potential. And it is vital to point them to the Source of all true joy and hope, Jesus Christ.

Jack was very vulnerable in these years. He wrote of how no one took time with him to place Christianity in its context. He immersed himself in the writing of the influential Roman poet Virgil, much favoured by the Roman Emperor Caesar Augustus. Virgil's qualities of tenderness, humanity, and deep religious sentiment prefigured Christianity; but there was no one who took the time to show Jack that what the pagans had longed for, or aspired to, was fulfilled in Christ. Christianity was taught to him as being true, but no one really attempted to show him why. A Nazi regime was about to rise up in Europe. The story is told of a prisoner in desperate thirst, who reached out to break off and suck an icicle. A guard smashed the icicle in front of him. The prisoner turned to the guard and asked, "Why?" "Here there is no why," he answered. We must all be allowed to ask, "Why?"

In Isaiah we read the words of God as He pleads, "'Come now, let us reason together,' says the Lord, 'though your sins are like scarlet, they shall be white as snow; though they are red as crimson, they shall be like wool'" (Isaiah 1:18). God allows us to ask why. He also gives us answers.

The vulnerable Jack was now confronted with the God-Man and the men-gods. In a very real sense, he began to experience the truth of Benjamin Disraeli's words: "Man is made to adore and obey; but if you give him nothing to worship, he will fashion his own divinities and find a chieftain in his own passions."

Slowly but surely, Jack became an atheist. He was influenced by the argument of Lucretius:

Had God designed the world, it would not be
A world so frail and faulty as we see.

Because Jack's experience showed him a fractured world, he reckoned a perfect God could not have created it; so he gave up his belief in God altogether. As with any teenager, his sexuality began to assert itself. Jack struggled for some time with sexual temptation which produced sever guilt and despondency. His friend, George Sayer, has written about how Jack found very little spiritual support during this time from either his schoolmasters or the clergymen.[6]

In reaction to the guilt he was experiencing, Sayer explains, Jack now went in for "bravado, blasphemy, and smut, startling and even shocking the boys who knew him best."[7] He also fell under the influence of a young schoolteacher whom he called Pogo, who was somewhat like a P. G. Woodhouse character. He began to imitate this man-about-town, Pogo. He put a lot of emphasis upon clothes. He wore ties with pins in them, low-cut coats, loud socks, and brogue shoes. He became foppish, caddish, and snobbish. By now he was smoking regularly.

Were his days all misery? No, but he was generally pessimistic. For him, the time between his childhood and adolescence was a sort of Dark Ages. Throughout his childhood, his father had stressed the need for ceaseless work and struggle, else disaster would overtake one's life; this reminder only added to the gloom.

Jack and Warren's practise of smoking and reading magazines and books in the Lime Street Hotel in Liverpool, after arriving on the night ferry from Ireland, was a mild form of teenage rebellion against Albert and their school regime. They would sit in the hotel until the last possible train south to Malvern. Jack described his mind at this time as being vulgar. He acknowledged that he had lost his faith, his virtue, and his simplicity.

But he still looked forward to his school holidays. His father enjoyed the mixture of music and comedy acts at the Belfast Hippodrome on a Saturday night, but Jack, who accompanied him with Warren, had no relish for it. The Hippodrome, which is no more, was on Great Victoria Street. It was host to many famous stars, including Sir Harry Lauder. General Booth of the Salvation Army preached there on 19 June 1908 in front of a crowd of fifteen hundred. It cost £5 to hire the Hippodrome; and, according to the Salvation Army Adjutant to the Belfast Citadel, that cost was too high, and the offering did not meet the extra expense!

The famous theatre and its shows did not capture young Jack Lewis half as much as did the glorious supper that awaited him on his return to Little Lea at around ten o'clock. He was back in the land of porridge that sticks to your ribs; of newly-baked soda bread, split while still warm and served with lashings of butter and strawberry jam; and Ulster's wheaten bread, a version of soda bread, made with whole wheat flour. The cook at Little Lea, Annie Strahan, was famous for her raised pies, and Jack relished them on a Saturday night. Baked in a mould (probably only to be seen now in National Trust houses) and eaten cold, those raised pies were a significant bite. Jack boasted that no modern English boy would have any idea of the pie and neither would the general public in Ulster. Annie's pies were much better than the ones sold in the shops. Ulster's tradition of fine home cooking continues in the twenty-first century. To Jack, Annie Strahan's cooking was the best he ever tasted.

If Annie's comforting pies lifted his spirits, the departure of Miss Cowie from Cherbourg did not. She was harshly dismissed for being found holding Jack in her arms—something she did with the boys in the school, and with total motherly innocence. She was sacked also for siding with Jack when he objected to his letters being censored by a schoolmaster. Miss Cowie may have unwittingly brought evil into Jack's life, but she also brought much good. As a highly sensitive teenager, he was touched deeply by her absence. The additional departure of a male teacher whom he had liked added to his sense of loss.

Were there any gems that appeared during Jack's Dark Ages? There was certainly a very memorable one. We have already discovered that the word which Jack used for his inner imaginative world was "Northerness." He loved the counties of Down, Antrim, Londonderry, and later County Donegal, because they were more "Northern." Soon he came under the influence of Wagner's *Ring,* which inspired him to write a remarkable heroic poem. In a Belfast music shop he found, gloriously, a gramophone record of the third act, *The Ride of the Valkyries.*

In his schoolroom Jack discovered a periodical with the title *Siegfried and the Twilight of the Gods.* Again, the words triggered his Northerness, and he was engulfed by "a vision of huge, clear spaces, hanging above the Atlantic in the endless twilight of Northern Summer, remoteness, severity."[8] The memory of joy came back, and how he longed to find it!

Jack's cousin Hope Ewart was now married and living in Dundrum outside Dublin. Jack was delighted when he found a complete copy of *Siegfried and the Twilight of the Gods,* illustrated by Arthur Rackham, in her home. Deeply coveting the book, he managed with Warren's help to get a cheaper copy at 7s6d. He cycled around the Wicklow Mountains, looking for scenes that might fit Wagner's world. Nature came to mean much more to him, bringing him joy. He wrote that for him joy was always a desire for something in the past, further away, or still to come. Even the mood of a natural scene became important to him; its smell and touch were vital. He began to read widely about Norse mythology, but he believed the gods he found there to be false.

God does not allow everything in our unconverted days to go to waste. Despite Jack's faults, God was working in his life, teaching him something of the nature of worship. In time he came to believe fervently that we should thank God more for who He is than for what He does for us. As the great Searcher of Souls sought out Jack Lewis, He taught him many lessons. One day the glory of God would uniquely capture his heart and mind; God would draw him from the false to the true, and Jack would know how to communicate the difference to millions of people. The Creator of great things was moulding this Northern writer for even greater things.

Jack later regretted his teenage apostasy; but in the far country the prodigal learned what his Heavenly Father's heart was truly like. One day, the High Gates would be opened to him.

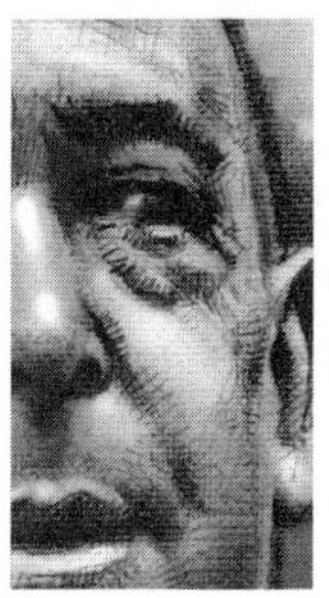

Chapter Six

THE GATES OF HIS SECLUSION

In September 1913 the seed-eating birds of Britain, such as the goldfinch and linnet, were feasting on the seedling thistle-heads. As the fields were being ploughed, the lapwings were crying along with the screeching black-headed gulls behind the plough. Missel thrushes were feeding in the tops of the tall bushes. Robins were back, their sweet, clear little songs ringing out as they searched for worms in the newly turned potato plots.

The time of migration from Britain's shores had come. The cuckoo had gone at the end of July, followed by the nightingale in August. A search across the country would have revealed that the willow and reed warblers, the black cap, and even the little chiffchaff could no longer be heard singing in the lanes and woods. They had responded to the call from other shores.

The lines from telegraph poles in villages, towns, and cities were threaded like pearl strings with swallows. With their domestic cares slackened, the swallows raised a sweet and melodic song that was extremely soothing to the ear. In the blue vault of the sky above Malvern, they were wheeling in ever widening circles. As the air grew colder, the insect life for which they were hawking was getting thinner. Soon there would be a hint of frost in the air, and the swallows would be off to Africa. They did not intend to spend the winter in England.

There was no such escape for Jack. From September 1913 to July 1914 he attended Malvern College; and such was his misery that it was only when he threatened to shoot himself that his father took him away. Although he was to later admit that his description of Malvern in his autobiography was overcharged, nonetheless his unhappiness there was acute.

One of the very first duties required of him at Malvern was to find out what Club he was in. The Club was a unit to which boys were consigned for compulsory games. When Lewis found the notice board where the Club lists were posted, it was surrounded by a crowd of boys further up the hierarchy in the college. He had to squeeze himself through the crowd and then face the task of reading through five hundred names to find his own. He had only ten minutes before he had to fulfil another important task and was forced away from the board. He went back to his college house sweating. It was a great relief when a boy to whom he gave the nickname Freeble shouted that he could tell Jack his Club, since it was the one to which he, Freeble, also belonged. It was B6. Jack felt hugely privileged that Freeble should condescend to help him. On half-holidays, when Jack went to the B6 notice board to see whether his name was down to play that afternoon, he discovered with joy that it never was. He truly hated games.

It was not until several weeks had passed that Jack discovered Freeble had lied. Jack's name had appeared several times on another notice board, and he was now accused of skipping Clubs. As punishment the head of the college flogged him in the presence of the assembled prefects. Summoned to his flogging by a boy who was the emissary for the college president, Jack was told in no uncertain terms that he was a nobody and that the college president was the most important person that existed. It was not a joyful beginning to life at Malvern College. He had gone there full of excitement and expectations. The athletes and prefects of Malvern were called Bloods, and he had held them in awe. As the governing class of Malvern, they had seemed like gods to him. They were a privileged hierarchy; and now he learned from them that he was a nobody.

On his first day Jack was sent to sit with about a dozen new boys in a large, dark room. They felt apprehensive and talked in whispers as they sat on a bench around a table clamped to the floor. They were all waiting to see if they would be among the few chosen to be given a real study. As he waited, Jack began to notice that serious moral problems existed in his new academic setting. He discovered that very questionable practises existed among some of the older boys in their interaction with the new students.

In his autobiography, with irony and sarcasm, Jack poured scorn on the public school system as he found it. Understandably, he did not think it came up to its aim, to prepare boys for public life. Others who knew Malvern around Jack's time think he exaggerated about the conditions but admit that homosexual practises did in fact exist among the students. It would be wrong to judge the English public school system solely on Jack's view of it. A more balanced view has been portrayed by R. F. Delderfield's novel *To Serve Them All My Days*, published in 1971.

Jack grew to hate the elitism he found in the Public School System. He regarded the social climbing and orthodoxy within its conventions as spiritually deadening. These deadening influences persisted from a child's first day at school. Watching the nervous strain of boys as they went out to be coached at games, feeling that their very future depended on their performance, Jack could not subscribe to the glorified position the games were given in the schools. That he himself was no good at games was beside the point!

At Malvern a House Master's signature was necessary if one was to be excused from playing in a compulsory game. So forgers emerged, and forging signatures made them steady pocket money. All elements of playing a game simply for the sake of playing were removed. Boys even patrolled the crowds at matches, to make sure that anyone whose support was not enthusiastic enough was duly punished.

Of all the boys attending Malvern at this time, one untamable Irish Earl defied its oligarchy. By night the pipe-smoking Earl slinked off without permission to a neighbouring city, always carrying a revolver. His habit was to load only one chamber of the gun. At times he would rush into a boy's study and, pointing the revolver at him, fire off all the empty chambers. A boy's life depended on the Earl's accurate counting. Jack called him Ballygunnian, and liked him because he didn't care about not being part of the Malvern pecking order.

Jack came to hate Malvern. Outwardly, he could cover up his misery, loneliness, and sense of desolation, just as he had hidden his loathing of adult parties in East Belfast. He could flow along, with the help of his storytelling and mimicry of people, especially teachers. There was lots of pretence, grimacing, slinking, and evasion. He was often told to "take that look off your face." Whatever look he had assumed, and however smutty and foul his language was at times, it all hid a deep unhappiness.

Of course, as always, he had his better moments. He excelled in much of his schoolwork. In his first term, within a few weeks of his arrival on 19 October, he was sent to the Headmaster—not for breaking a rule or for skipping a Club, but for writing an outstanding poem entitled *Carpe Diem? After Horace*. By all accounts it was a masterpiece for a boy of his age.

Beyond his best expectation and hope, at Malvern Jack had one of the greatest teachers that he would ever know. A friend of the great English composer Sir Edward Elgar, Harry Wakelyn Smith was Jack's Form Master. He was fifty-four years of age, an eccentric, with grey hair, a white moustache, large spectacles, and a wide mouth. He was thin and wore a billowing gown, an old fashioned turned-up collar, and a bootlace tie. He called his pupils "gentlemen," and treated them as such. In turn they responded by behaving like gentlemen in his class. This well-mannered, courteous, brilliant schoolmaster, known to the boys as Smugy, took up where Lewis Alden of Campbell College had left off.

Smugy had an outstanding gift for reading poetry. He had a tongue that seemed to be touched with honey, and his poetry-reading style fell between speech and song. Smugy's enchanting reading was to influence the way Jack Lewis read poetry for the rest of his life. The cadence of Smugy's voice, his sensitive ear for the music of poetry, the gentlemanly manner of his teaching, and his great ability to analyse the grammar and syntax of a poem, were meat and drink to the scared, lonely misfit that was the fifteen-year-old Jack Lewis. Smugy would invite groups of boys to his house for tea; and in class he would take time to sit beside each boy to have an individual conversation with him, advising and encouraging him. Despite the soaring emotions Smugy released in his readings, he was a stickler for scholarly detail. When he read a poem, syntax and beauty were synonyms. He made accuracy a bulwark against uncouthness. He also made Jack's year at Malvern more bearable.

Another sanctuary for Jack's troubled spirit was what was known as "The Grundy," the school library. A boy was not faggable when he was inside the library. Within public schools in England, fagging was a system whereby younger boys acted as servants to the older boys. Duties ranged from keeping the older boy's kit clean and tidy, to helping him with his exam revision. In return the senior boy was supposed to protect the youngster. Fagging was supported because it was thought to encourage an ethos of service similar to that found in the army and navy. It was seen as a means of instituting group conformity and loyalty. The general bullying of weaker boys by those older or stronger was seen as preparing boys for manhood and leadership. It also helped to save the school the expense of employing more domestic servants. In the United States the word "fagging" is now used as derogatory slang; but the original meaning of the word "fag" is "weary," and refers to a tiring or unwelcome task. In English, to be "fagged out" still means to be exhausted.

With all the rest of his contemporaries, Jack had his share of fagging. With it came the responsibility of making a Blood's tea, cleaning out his study, or, most onerous of all, cleaning his boots. Jack had to obey a Blood's orders immediately, although Jack had been placed in a high form, had a lot of work to do, and could ill afford the time. When called upon, Jack had to fag as a shoeblack. That job involved waiting in the queue behind other fags in a smelly, cold, dark cellar to take his turn at the appropriate brushes and shoe polish. The job would interrupt the precious time between breakfast and morning school, when he wanted to go over set passages of translation with the boys in his form. To escape fagging, the Grundy was bliss. To avoid Bloods on the way to the library was not easy. Meeting one could cost him his afternoon.

It was in the Grundy that Jack discovered the mythical poetry of his fellow Irishman W. B. Yeats; and a book on Celtic mythology became almost as great a feeder of his imagination as Norse mythology had become earlier. He also came to love Greek mythology with its sun-kissed stories, so very different from the Northern skies he treasured. He attempted to write an epic poem on the Irish legends Cuchulain and Finn; his Northerness still triumphed over the other two cultures. He wrote a play—an opera libretto—called *Loki Bound* that was Norse in subject and in Greek form. In the play, Loki was a projection of himself, and Thor was the villain, a symbol of the Bloods in his school. Loki was against the deity called Odin, because Odin had created a world; and Loki thought it was cruel that creatures should have the burden of existence forced upon them without their consent. Through his play Jack was showing that he was angry with God for creating a world in which he carried the burden of existence without having asked for it. So far it had often been a very miserable existence indeed for Jack, and it would get worse. As he sat in the silence of the Grundy, soaking up the books, listening to the bees buzzing by the open windows and the sound of leather on willow from a distant cricket match, a treacherous tide was lapping to the shores of his seclusion.

"The careful assignments of School Masters were blotted out by larger and wider markings," wrote James Hilton, author of the novel *Goodbye, Mr. Chips*.

> A boy who had been expelled returned as a hero with medals; those whose inability to conjugate *avoir* and *être* seemed

> likely in 1913 to imperil a career were to conquer France's enemies better than they did her language; offenders gated for cigarette smoking in January were dropping bombs from the sky in December. It was a frantic world: and we knew it even if we did not talk about it. Slowly, inch by inch, the tide of war lapped to the gates of our seclusion.[1]

The sad fact was that few of the 1912-1913 Malvern College boys would return from Flanders with medals. Most of them, including the untamable Irish Earl, were slaughtered. The poetry would be "in the pity,"[2] wrote the great First World War poet Wilfred Owen. In his "Anthem for Doomed Youth," he wrote:

What passing-bells for these who die as cattle?
Only the monstrous anger of the guns.
Only the stuttering rifles' rapid rattle
Can patter out their hasty orisons.
No mockeries for them from prayers nor bells,
Nor any voice of mourning save the choirs, –
The shrill, demented choirs of wailing shells;
And bugles calling for them from sad shires.[3]

As the tide of war came closer and closer, the teenager from Ulster was caught in a duality of outer and inner life. Outwardly he felt misery, but in his spirit he was touched at times by unspeakable moments of happiness. These came from a deep awareness of the beauty of nature and from the world of books and imagination. The conclusion Jack came to of his time at Malvern was that, in hindsight, he was extremely tired—tired as a cab horse. His work, the pressures of life under the fagging system, and the whole strain of growing up had exhausted him. He also concluded that he had become a downright intellectual prig. The Enemy had been busy; and as always he had left neither peace of heart nor peace of mind behind him. But the voice of something indescribably beautiful was about to speak to Jack; he was to call it the Voice of Holiness.

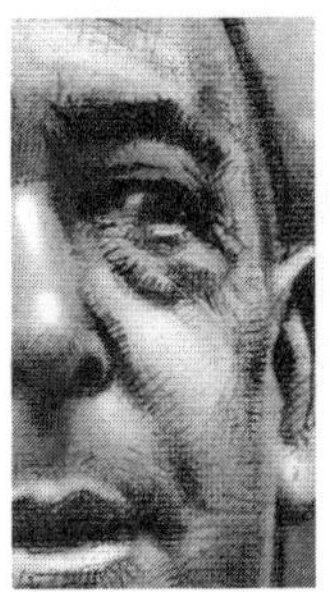

Chapter Seven

NO CALLING WITHOUT A CALLER

The orchards of England were overflowing with fruit. Deep red and yellow streaked apples, dusky skinned plums, and russet coloured pears filled the most heavily wooded county in England, namely Surrey. Its forests contained a wide range of trees—oak, pine, beech, sweet chestnut, juniper, yew, and ash. Some of those woodlands had been in existence since before AD 1600. From the chalk grasslands of the North Downs to the heaths of the London Basin, Surrey was a county of remarkable natural beauty.

Much of Surrey's fruit had already been gathered; but a sleepless person listening carefully on moonlit nights could have heard the thud of the ripened fruit falling to the orchard floor. Across the county butterflies flitted, especially the heath-loving butterflies, to the delight of all who saw them. Their colours ranged from red to chalk-blue, from grey and brown to white and copper. Any rambler could have disturbed them by his or her footstep.

Jack's journey from Belfast to Great Bookham in September 1914 was a feast for his eyes. As he walked the paths and lanes of Surrey, he grew to love its countryside with its abundant woodland plants. He revelled in its coppices, woods, and hollows, and enjoyed its heather, gorse, and bracken. He was to know as much happiness in Surrey as he was ever to know on earth.

What had brought about this great turn-around? Where now was the misery of the Ulster misfit, his detestation of the Public School system, the multi-layered anxiety of the growing boy? The answer was in the tall, lean, gentleman who stood waiting for Jack at Great Bookham Station, dressed, as always, in worn-out clothes. His name was William Thompson Kirkpatrick. The former Headmaster of Lurgan College, now living in semi-retirement, took on one or two pupils for private tuition. From September to December 1915, after Warren's disastrous academic career at Malvern, Mr. Kirkpatrick had tutored Warren. Mr. Kirkpatrick turned Warren's education around. When Warren sat his entrance examination for the army he was placed twenty-first out of 201 candidates and entered the Royal Military Academy at Sandhurst as a prize candidate in February 1914. Warren advised his father to send Jack to Great Bookham and Mr. Kirkpatrick, and Jack never stopped pleading with his father, by pen and tongue, to take him away from Malvern. Through doubt and hesitation, Albert finally made up his mind to let Jack read for University under the tuition of Mr. Kirkpatrick. Jack looked upon the decision as, humanly speaking, the most fortunate thing that had ever happened to him.

Jack had expected Mr. Kirkpatrick to be a sentimental person. He had heard his father speak of him in such terms, and Jack almost anticipated being hugged by him on arrival. He was in for a shock: a less sentimental teacher had never existed.

Mr. Kirkpatrick shook Jack's hand firmly, and as they walked away from the station Jack tried to make conversation with him. He mentioned that he had found the landscape of Surrey to be much wilder than he had expected. Mr. Kirkpatrick immediately shouted, "Stop!" He asked Jack to explain what he meant by wildness, and on what grounds he had not expected it. Mr. Kirkpatrick demolished all of Jack's answers to the point at which he asked Jack if he could not see that his remark had been meaningless! Mr. Kirkpatrick did not stop there, but tried to ferret out what Jack's expectations had been based upon. Had he seen maps of Surrey, photographs, or books? Mr. Kirkpatrick's conclusion was that Jack did not have any right to an opinion on the subject, due to the fact that he could not produce proof of anything upon which his stated opinion was based. All of this first conversation took place in the space of three and a half minutes; but it set the sail for the rest of Jack's voyage through two and a half years at Great Bookham.

In a nutshell, W. T. Kirkpatrick taught Jack logic—a process that he simply loved. No doubt Jack inherited this love from his mother. He was no mathematician when it came to calculation, but he did delight in reasoning. Jack, his father, and Warren called Mr. Kirkpatrick "The Great Knock." I surmise that this title encapsulated how Mr. Kirkpatrick was able to "knock" an argument. This ability marked him in every aspect of his social conversation. He even demanded that his wife's elderly bridge partners clarify their terms!

The Great Knock's influence on Jack marked him for the rest of his life. Using Mr. Kirkpatrick's technique, he soon learned to reason and argue, to formidable effect. "Fame is a vapour, popularity an accident, riches take wing, and only character endures," said Horace Greeley. Through Mr. Kirkpatrick, the logic of Jack's character became in-built, enduring to this day. And how! His devastating logic would deeply influence his students at Oxford and Cambridge Universities. Through his books untold millions of people would be touched. It is estimated that his books have sold 200 million copies, making him the best-selling Christian author of all time. Three-dozen titles are still in print. At the height of the war, millions would listen to the radio as Jack the apologist spoke in defence of the Christian faith. Multitudes of children would learn of Christ through that logic, used in his creative way.

Consider for a moment the fifteen-year-old Jack Lewis being taught logic in the Kirkpatrick home at Great Bookham in the years 1914 to 1916. Jack is a pessimist and an atheist. His teacher is also an atheist. Mr. Kirkpatrick once studied in a Presbyterian seminary; but the only visible trace of his Ulster Protestant past is that he wears more respectable clothes while gardening on Sunday than he does on other days of the week. So, if ever William Cowper's famous line, "God moves in a mysterious way, His wonders to perform" were shown to be true, this was the time. An atheist teaches another atheist how to use logic; and ever since Lewis's conversion, God has been using the logic of this former atheist behind enemy lines to devastating effect. God does as He pleases, when He pleases, where He pleases, how He pleases, and with whom He pleases. "Let no one get a swelled head if the Lord uses them," said Stuart Briscoe, "for He uses some mighty strange people."

Of course, Mr. Kirkpatrick taught Jack far more than logic. Soon he was able not only to read Greek; he could think in Greek. All of this knowledge was passed on to Jack in a pure, unadulterated Ulster accent. The *Iliad*, read by the The Great Knock, may not have been in as honeyed an accent as Smugy's; but to Jack it suited the Bronze Age in which it was written.

Jack's time at Great Bookham fell into a very pleasant pattern. It was a pattern he tried to continue; but it was often interrupted by life and its responsibilities. Breakfast, with Mrs. Kirkpatrick's good Ulster soda bread, was at eight o'clock a.m. By nine o'clock a.m. Jack was working at his desk with Mr. Kirkpatrick in a little upstairs study. He read and wrote until one o'clock p.m., happily interrupted by a cup of tea or coffee from Mrs. Kirkpatrick at eleven o'clock a.m. After lunch, he went for a walk at around two o'clock p.m., usually alone. His sense of nature and its moods was acute, and he found talk irritating as he drank in the beauty of the Surrey countryside. He advised any walker in the countryside to keep his mouth shut and his eyes and ears opened. One needed to surrender to nature to enjoy it. Afternoon tea was not later than 4.15 p.m., often taken alone, musing over an ever-present book. Jack loved to read while he ate; not many sixteen-year-olds today would be found musing on Lang's *History of English Literature,* reading a translation of Herodotus, or enjoying the writing of Boswell over afternoon tea. Jack would work until the evening meal at seven o'clock p.m. There followed French with Mrs. Kirkpatrick, talk, or further light reading. He was usually in bed by eleven o'clock p.m.

This was Jack's model for a normal day, though he described it as selfish and Epicurean. Epicureans taught that pleasure, particularly mental pleasure, was the highest good; and Jack had plenty of that at Great Bookham. Life would soon interrupt this pattern in a thousand ways, but Jack found truly great happiness in the peace and quietness of the daily routine in the Kirkpatrick household. At Great Bookham, Jack was not exposed to material wealth. If anything, the household was somewhat frugal. This frugality was perhaps best epitomised in The Great Knock's habit of rising abruptly from the table and going to an old tobacco jar to rescue remnants of tobacco from former pipes for use again. What Jack found at Great Bookham was a wealth of intellectual pleasure; when he describes the arrival of books in little dark grey paper parcels from Messrs. Denny in The Strand, London, one can almost feel his joy. His reading list at Great Bookham stretches across intellectual continents: Milton, Keats, Shelley, Chaucer, Lang, Stephens, Malory, Sir Walter Scott, Spenser, Sidney, Ronsard, Voltaire, Walton, Mandeville, William Morris, Apuleius, Herrick, Ruskin, the Brontes, Demosthenes, Cicero, Lucretius, Tacitus, Virgil, Maeterlinck, Yeats, Wilde, and Beardsley. Where did it all lead him? What of Jack's spiritual well being at Great Bookham? Who influenced him most?

It turns out that one of the deepest influences was the poet W. B. Yeats. Jack soon discovered that Yeats seriously believed in magic. Jack was to meet him later in life and to have that fact confirmed. As we have noted already, Yeats was deeply into the occult; and Jack, who had by now discarded Christianity, found Yeats' belief in another world disturbing. Through further reading of Maeterlinck—with his spiritualism, theosophy, and pantheism—an old, ravenous desire for the occult, first aroused by Miss Cowie the matron at Malvern, rushed into his soul. In that same soul, however, at the same time, another desire arose. It was the longing for what he had known, in his childhood, of joy. Without hesitation, he admitted that the first desire came from the Devil. To Jack, the nature of joy was not coarse, as the occult was. His teenage experiences and temptations had absolutely no relevance to those incredible experiences of joy he had known in childhood. He had discovered early that the world, the flesh, and the Devil could not give him joy. It was a mercy that he made the discovery; and he was just about to make another.

In the Scriptures, we read of God's intervening in the history of the world through tiny incidents. The beautiful Rebekah goes down to a spring with a jar on her shoulder. "Please give me a little water from your jar," says Eliezer, Abraham's servant. She gives it to him and adds, "I'll draw water for your camels, too." Her act led to her marriage to Isaac and the protection of the royal line of the Messiah. For Rebekah, her action was merely watering thirsty camels; but it was more, so very much more.

Later in history, a little baby is found crying. What could be more common? From the tears of baby Moses, though, flows the tide of the history of Israel. His tears evoked compassion in Pharaoh's daughter, and Moses was raised as her son. History shows that Moses was educated in the sciences: mathematics, astronomy, chemistry, medicine, philosophy, and law. He was trained in the arts: music, sculpture, and painting. He was taught the protocol of kings, covering the fifteen-hundred-year history of Egypt's existence. He knew the secrets of the pyramids. In order to free Moses' own people from the cruel slavery imposed by Pharaoh, God reached into the very family of Pharaoh. The baby who had wept led 2.5 million people to freedom through the Red Sea. Think about that fact the next time you hear a baby cry!

Ruth, the poverty-stricken, barley-gleaning Moabitess "happened" to come to that part of a Bethlehem field belonging to a man called Boaz. The seeming happenstance led to romance and marriage. Ruth's great-grandson was called David—arguably the greatest poet who ever lived. From that royal line came the Messiah, who was called David's Greater Son. And all hung on Ruth's going into one part of a field instead of another.

Paul decided to visit churches he had founded, simply to encourage them. Step by step, he was led to a women's prayer meeting by the side of a river in Philippi. He sat down and shared the gospel with the women in what was the first Christian service to be held in Europe. One of their number, a businesswoman from Thyatira called Lydia, *whose heart the Lord opened*, invited Paul to her home. So God opened Lydia's heart; then He opened her home; and then He opened a continent to the gospel. A woman's heart was God's highway to Europe.

In life, what appears to have small beginnings can lead to incredible ends. A NASA astrophysicist told me one day on a jet from Washington to London, "We can prove that butterflies, moving their wings in India, affect the weather in North America." You could have fooled me!

One awesome evening at twilight on Leatherhead Station platform in Surrey, the door to a new world opened for Jack Lewis. He usually walked to Leatherhead about once a week to have a bathe in the small swimming pool, to look for books, or to get his hair cut; and he took the train back. As he stood with one lone porter on the timbered platform waiting for the train to arrive, his ears tingling with the cold, he turned to the station bookstall. The sky, he would always remember, was green with frost and the Dorking Hills were almost violet in colour. There, lying on the bookstall, in a soiled jacket, was a cheap Everyman edition of a book called *Phantastes: A Faerie Romance for Men and Women*. The author was George MacDonald. Almost unwillingly Jack bought the book as the steam train arrived slowly. "Bookham, Effingham, Horsley," called the porter, and Jack Lewis got on board. As the train headed into the gathering darkness, the growing boy, though he did not know it, was heading towards the light. For that night he began reading his new book, which had cost him 1s1d.

George MacDonald (1824-1905), born in Huntley, Aberdeenshire, was a distinctly gifted Christian gentleman. He was a poet, a novelist, and a fantasy writer *par excellence*; he was a highly successful lecturer, actor, editor, teacher, and preacher; and he was a husband and the father of eleven children. He wrote fifty books, thirty of them novels, which have sold millions of copies. His books never brought him wealth; his novels in particular reflect insights born out of a life of near poverty and poor health. In the midst of it all, he had experienced the touch and blessing of God. George MacDonald was a friend of Lady Byron (the poet's widow), Charles Kingsley, John Ruskin, Mark Twain, Henry Wadsworth Longfellow, Matthew Arnold, Lewis Carroll, and other literary figures. If you ever walk in Hyde Park and see the statue of the boy and dolphin, it is worth remembering that the sculptor was Matthew Monroe, George MacDonald's friend. Monroe used George MacDonald's son Greville as a model for his statue. Smith Elder published *Phantastes: A Faerie Romance for Men and Women* in 1848. It had taken two months to write. George Murray Smith, the head of the publishing company, had been the first person to recognise the genius of Charlotte Bronte's *Jane Eyre*; he also recognised *Phantastes'* unique place in English literature. The book certainly found a unique place in Jack's heart.

What was it that touched him? MacDonald said that his book was a sort of fairy tale for grown people. It is generally agreed that it is not an easy book to grasp; it is full of mythical fantasy and symbolic dream-romance. It is an allegory of the spiritual pilgrimage out of this temporal world into the Kingdom of Heaven. At this stage in his life, Jack had discarded Christianity. He believed that, just as humankind had deified the sun and the moon, so it deified great people. He believed that Jesus was a Hebrew philosopher who had been deified, that the Christian church was a cult, and that Christian truth was superstitious faith. He believed all religions to be mythologies. All these beliefs he had hidden from his father; for the sake of convention, he had even travelled to Belfast from Surrey to be confirmed in the Church of Ireland. In time, however, he admitted to being ashamed of his insincerity.

Within hours of reading *Phantastes*, though, something strangely new and invigorating began to touch his imagination. Almost daily he enjoyed the woodland air of the beautiful Surrey countryside, but when he began journeying in *Phantastes*, he felt he was breathing a new air. He called it a sweet air that blew from the land of righteousness. Here was cool, morning innocence; here was goodness. Unknowingly, he had crossed a frontier; he had been carried across it, he admitted, as if he were asleep.

Jack had been charmed and lured by the imaginative worlds of Malory, Spenser, Maurice, and Yeats; but now he was attracted by something completely different. It was called holiness. He described it as being like the sun breaking through fog. It created a bright shadow that touched and transformed everything around him. It was the Divine touching the everyday and ordinary. It was the spiritual touching the material.

Holiness is lovely. Of course, it opposes and exposes sin. Holiness is opposed to sin, just as a doctor is opposed to disease—but with the aim of making the patient whole. What hope has God of making us holy? The answer is that, because of Christ's death, His resurrection, and His return to His Father, all who repent toward God and put faith in Jesus Christ have the experience of the Holy Spirit's entering their lives. Satan's ultimate intention, to block Christ's work of making sinners holy, is thus defeated. That same Holy Spirit was convicting Jack Lewis, and He used George MacDonald's writing to show him that the Enemy had sold him erotic and mystical perversions of joy. It was a profound revelation that would continue to influence him for the rest of his life. As he later stated, C. S. Lewis never concealed the fact that he regarded George MacDonald as his master.

Towards the time of his death, George MacDonald suffered acutely. At that time he wrote the following verses. Though the original verses were left in an unpolished state, they show the heart that forty years later spoke to Jack's heart. As Jack was to learn, George MacDonald saw that Christ was truly the "heart of all joy below, above." These verses are amongst the most precious anyone could read:

Come through the gloom of clouded skies,
The slow dim rain and fog athwart,
Through East winds keen and wrong and lies,
Come and make strong my hopeless heart.

Come through the sickness and the pain,
The sore unrest that tosses still,
The aching dark that hides the gain –
Come and arouse my fainting will.

Through all the fears—that spirits bow –
Of what hath been or may befall,
Come down and talk with me, for thou
Canst tell me all about them all

Come, Lord of Life—here is thy seat,
Heart of all joy below, above –
One minute let me kiss thy feet
And name the names of those I love.[1]

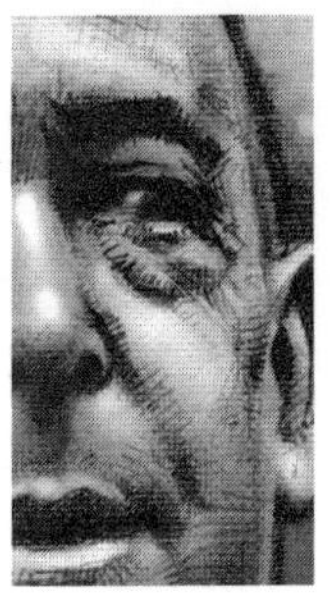

Chapter Eight

OXFORD IN MANTLING SNOW

The butterfish wriggled and the mustard-coloured lichens continued to roughen the black rocks along the County Down coast. The salt air, the summer sun, and the sandy soil of the coast were favourable to the flourishing wild rhododendrons. The bees hummed in the veronica and among the fuchsia hedges, so profuse along the roadsides of the Ards Peninsula. Above the town of Newtownards on Scrabo Hill stood Scrabo Tower. Charles Lanyon designed and built it in 1857 in memory of the third Marquis of Londonderry, who had been kind to the people during the potato famine. Lord Londonderry had commanded a brigade of hussars under the famous Sir John Moore in the Peninsular Wars against Napoleon.

The tower looked away to Strangford Lough, with its seventy islets just as the glaciers had left them. The area was a haven for brent geese, dunlins, oystercatchers, mallards and widgeons, gulls and cormorants. The streams of County Down were the habitat of the busy water spider, who knew the concept of the diving bell long before man had ever conceived of the idea. The water spider carries air bubbles on the short downy hairs of its body, beneath the surface of water to a tiny store moored to the stalks of water plants. It is there that he makes his home and raises his family. In the pools of the county, water spiders, water beetles, and water crickets were about in their myriads; interestingly, almost every insect on land had its counterpart in water. Dragonflies, once grubs in the mud of the pools, were now flashing their incredible colours amongst the flowers of summer. The air was heavy with the scents of honeysuckle and pollen. And the tower looked away to what Jack Lewis called "the thing itself, utterly irresistible, the way to the world's end, the land of longing, the breaking and blessing of hearts." It was "the plain of Down, and seeing beyond it the Mourne Mountains."[1]

It was the summer of 1916, and Jack relished every minute of it. On this, as on other recent summers, he had traversed his main haunt, the Holywood Hills. These stood in an irregular line drawn from Stormont to Comber, Comber to Newtownards, Newtownards to Scrabo, Scrabo to Craigantlet, Craigantlet to Holywood, Holywood to Knocknagoney and back to Stormont. Often Jack walked with his new companion, Arthur Greeves, a man who was to be his friend for half a century.

Arthur lived at Bernagh, directly across the road from Little Lea. For years he had tried unsuccessfully to make friends with Warren and Jack. But shortly before starting his last term at Malvern, Jack received a message saying that Arthur was in bed convalescing and would be glad to see him. Jack responded to the invitation and went over to Bernagh to find Arthur sitting up in bed. On a table beside him lay a copy of the book *Myths of Norsemen* by H. A. Grueber. To their delight, Jack and Arthur discovered that they had a mutual passion for Scandinavian folklore. Jack was not the only boy on the Circular Road with a sense of Northerness. The grand and tragic mythology of Scandinavia was the bridge that the boys crossed to friendship. Arthur encouraged Jack to read classic English novels, including those by Jane Austen, the Brontës, Anthony Trollope, Elizabeth Gaskell, and Sir Walter Scott. Jack, in turn, encouraged Arthur's artistic talent. It was because of Jack's influence that Arthur studied at the Slade School of Fine Art in London from 1921 to 1923. Arthur proved to be an outstandingly loyal friend to Jack. He wisely kept secret the problems Jack shared with him concerning Jack's struggles during his adolescence.

Arthur and Jack loved to share walks together in the Holywood Hills area. With an artist's eye for detail and perspective, Arthur would point out, through a hole in a hedge, a farm in the mid-morning sunshine. He would point out drills of cabbages, or a grey cat squeezing under a barn door, or local characters going about their work. Arthur and Jack walked together in sunlight and moonlight, relishing the perfume of newly mown hay or watching the gulls wheeling and screaming around the furrows left by a ploughman. As far as they were concerned, their haunt was acre after acre of beauty, delight, and goodness.

Unquestionably, County Down is a county that deeply influenced Jack's imagination. It is a county of wildflowers, hips, haws, and wild mushrooms. In season, it is saturated with blackberries and hawthorns, all growing against a background of butterflies; the cooing of pigeons is in its forests and dragonflies are on the surface of its streams and lakes. Here was a county covered with the white dots of cottages which, Jack said, "laughed." And it all flowed on to the Mourne Mountains: to Slieve Donard, to

Deer's Meadow and the Hare's Gap, to the Brandy Pad, the Cock and Hen, Butter Mountain, the Rowan Tree River, to Crocknafeola and Slievemageough. Up near Lough Shannagh rose the River Bann, making its way past Rathfriland, Banbridge, Gilford, and Portadown, to Lough Neagh, and on to reach the sea at Castlerock under those Northern skies of Jack's early childhood. On the other side of the Mournes, of course, lay the enchanting Rostrevor-Carlingford area, which was to be the inspiration for *Narnia*. Its mixture of sea, woods, and mountains comprised what Jack reckoned to be the loveliest spot he had ever seen.[2]

It is significant now to realise that while Jack walked the inspiring hills of County Down with Arthur Greeves in the summer of 1916, a disastrous loss of the finest manhood in Great Britain and Ireland was taking place at the Somme in France. The Somme offensive began on the morning of 1 July 1916, in which the British Expeditionary Force and the French Army attempted to take the strong defensive position held by the Germans in the Somme Valley. Before the offensive was over, it is estimated, the British suffered 420,000 casualties, the French 200,000, and the Germans 500,000. It was one of the greatest tragedies in British history.

In the first two days of the battle, the thirty-sixth Ulster Division suffered 5,104 casualties, out of which approximately 2,069 died. The British troops had confidently set out into "no man's land" expecting to meet little resistance from their battered opponents, who had suffered one and a half million shells raining down on them in the eight days before the attack. But the German concrete bunkers were deep; their razor wire was unaffected by the bombardment; and their machine guns and rifles covered the entirety of "no man's land" in an arc. The Germans mowed their enemy down like grass. When the thirty-sixth Ulster Division was demobilised in 1919, it had suffered 32,000 casualties.

The effect of this holocaust on Ulster life was never better caught than in Rev. W. F. Marshall's poem *The Lad*. It tells the story of the orphaned son of a poor Linen scutcher.[3] As the little boy grew to manhood under the care of the ploughman who raised him, he kept the heart of a child who has a huge affinity with nature. But the war called. The ploughman's soliloquy is haunting:[4]

I'm feelin' oul' since he went away,
An' my sight is gettin' dim;
I niver axed for to keep him back
When they needed men like him.
He's sleepin' now where the poppies grow,
In a coat that the bullets tore,
An' what's a wheen of medals to me
When my own wee lad's no more?[5]

How did Jack respond to the unfolding slaughter in Europe? He made a decision. In Ireland there was no compulsory enlistment to the British Army; Jack could have gone to an Irish university and escaped fighting in the war. But he decided to serve when he reached military age and to seek to enter Oxford University. If he were successful there, he knew, he would become eligible for military service one month after entering the University. Until then, he would treat the matter of military service much as he treated the necessity of returning to unhappy school days after school holidays: he would avoid letting the thought infiltrate his mind. He decided not to follow the news of battles in the newspaper, but simply to fight in them when the hour came. He didn't trust newspapers, and he disliked their vulgarity and sensationalism. He believed their battle information to be third-hand, and therefore distorted.

Arthur began a correspondence with Jack in June 1914, and for a number of years they wrote to each other every week. Few subjects escaped comment. Arthur saved nearly all of Jack's letters, which were published in 1979 as the book *They Stand Together*. Despite their differences—and there were many—Jack and Arthur certainly stood together. Arthur—somewhat dull, with a tendency to self-pity—was deeply artistic, though verbally inarticulate. Jack, the man with ideas and concepts, was garrulous, with an argumentative turn of mind. He was also often arrogant. Arthur, though, was full of charity. In these years, one of them had rejected the Christian message; the other had held to it. Throughout most of his life, Arthur was to paint his beloved County Down; and Jack was to write about it for his millions of readers. It is very heartening to note that their loyalty to each other never faltered.

In the summer of 1916, Jack left County Down once more for Great Bookham. From there, on 4 December, he travelled to Oxford to take an entrance scholarship exam in classics. Here was what Matthew Arnold called "that sweet City with her dreaming spires," famous across the world for her university and unique place in history. The River Thames could be safely forded here; indeed, the name of the city comes from the Oxon Forde that crossed the river at today's Folly Bridge. Within the city of Oxford, the River Thames becomes the River Isis. Oxford was an established town in the ninth century; and for over eight hundred years it has been the home of scholars. Here stands the Bodleian Library, one of the Copyright Libraries. By law, a copy of every newspaper and even leaflet that is printed in the United Kingdom must be sent here. This tradition goes back to 1610. Books cannot be borrowed here, for it is only a reading library. Even King Charles I was refused permission to borrow a book from the Bodleian. Surprisingly, there is no university campus as such to visit, because Oxford University is in fact made up of over thirty-five separate colleges, each with its own distinct history and tradition.

Here, for example, is Christ Church College, arguably the most famous college in Oxford University. The main entrance is the archway of Tom Tower, one of the most famous landmarks in Oxford. The bell in the tower is rung 101 times at 9.05 every evening. The tradition dates from the foundation of the college, when the bell rang once for each of the college's original students, to tell them to return to the college before the gates were locked. Here John Wesley studied, as well as Lewis Carroll, Albert Einstein, and more than a dozen British prime ministers. Inside the college is Christ Church Cathedral, the smallest cathedral in England.

Just off the High Street is Brasenose College, named after the College's original doorknocker, which was nicknamed "The Brazen Nose." In the twelfth century, anyone using it would be provided sanctuary if he were escaping from the law.

Here, too, is Merton College, famous for its medieval buildings, some of which are the oldest in the university. In Jack's day J. R. R. Tolkien was a student here.

Here at the eastern end of the High Street is St. Edmund Hall. Dating from 1190, it is the oldest academic building in the whole city. The Mohawk Chief Oronhyatekha studied medicine here in the 1860's. Here hangs art by one of Jack's favourite prose writers, William Morris.

Here is New College, which is certainly not new, because it was founded in 1379! Here studied William Spooner, inventor of spoonerisms (sentences with the sounds transposed to create a new and amusing meaning). He once said to a student, "You have hissed your mystery lectures and tasted a whole worm!"

On St. Aldate's Street, opposite Christ Church College, stands Pembroke College, with its beautiful renaissance-style chapel dating from the eighteenth century. Here studied the great lexicographer Dr. Samuel Johnson, who published the first *Dictionary of the English Language* in 1755. Here is the spire of the Church of St. Mary the Virgin, where the first university meetings were held in the twelfth century; and here is the tower of Magdalen College, famous because the Magdalen College Choir sings here at dawn every May Day.

When Jack stepped off the train in Oxford for the first time, however, he was disappointed with the scenery. As he walked farther, things got worse. As mean shop followed mean shop one after another, Jack began to wonder where all the fabled spires and towers of Oxford could be. As the city quickly began to recede, and he saw the open countryside ahead, he turned around and looked back. There it stood in all its glory: a cluster of spires and towers, virtually unequalled anywhere on earth as an icon of learning. After drinking it all in he walked back to the railway station, took a hansom cab, and asked the driver to take him some place where he could get rooms for a week. He found such a place on Mansfield Road.

Jack called his first walk in Oxford an allegory of his life. It seems to me that, just as he turned the wrong way at the railway station and walked away from the glory of Oxford, so he had turned the wrong way at what John Bunyan called "The Wicket Gate" that would have set him on the way to "The Celestial City." Jack had read *Pilgrim's Progress* and the famous conversation between Christian and Evangelist:

> Then said Evangelist, pointing with his finger over a very wide field, "Do you see yonder wicket-gate?" (Matthew 7:14).

> The man said "no." Then said the other, "Do you see yonder shining light?" (Psalm 119:105; 2 Peter 1:19). He said, "I think I do." Then said Evangelist, "Keep that bright light in your eye and go directly thereto, so shalt thou see the gate: at which, when thou knockest, it shall be told thee what thou shalt do."

Various people—including Mr. Pliable, Mr. Obstinate and, of course, Mr. Worldly Wise Man—tried to persuade Christian to turn aside. But he got to the Wicket Gate, and it led him to the Cross of Christ, where his burden rolled out of sight forever. The road to the Celestial City now stretched before him. On Jack's spiritual journey, he had made a wrong turning. These wrong turns were to lead him down many a mean street, on which he met many a persuader who would have been delighted with Jack's first prose work, *The Pilgrim's Regress*. Here Jack would point up characters like Mr. Enlightenment (representing nineteenth-century rationalism), Mr. Sensible (representing cultured worldliness), Mr. Broad (who is on the pilgrimage, but is friends with the world), and, of course, Mr. Humanist. In the book we come across the shires of Orgiastica, Behmenheim, Occultica, and Aesthetica. There is a straight path, which guides pilgrims past the City of Claptrap[6] (a distinctly useful Ulster word for "nonsense"!).

The day after his arrival in Oxford, mantling snow began to fall on the fabled city. Wearing a great coat and muffler, the eighteen-year-old Jack Lewis headed to the Hall of Oriel College, whose alumni include Sir Walter Raleigh and Cecil Rhodes. The young Ulsterman sitting his exam in the cold hall, his left hand in a glove, was busy writing an essay based on a quotation from one of the illustrious alumni of Pembroke College, Samuel Johnson. "What is written without effort is in general read without pleasure," Johnson had once commented. As for Jack, he gained no pleasure from what he had written, for he felt he had almost certainly failed.

When after a week of examinations he left the snow-covered Oxford and eventually headed home to Belfast for Christmas, he admitted to his father his fears over his exams. Albert Lewis sought to comfort his son with tender and kindly words. The Great Knock, on hearing the questions set for Jack, also presumed that he had done badly. His tutor felt the questions had not been suited to him. But both men were wrong. On 19 December, the Master of University College Oxford wrote to say that the College had awarded him the second of three open scholarships for classics.

There was one problem, though. Jack would have to pass a separate examination called Responsions that included one of Jack's weakest subjects, mathematics. He returned to The Great Knock for one final golden term and sat the examination in March. He failed, but he was allowed to enter his college at Oxford in April, with another Responsions examination in view. He entered his name in University College's books on 28 April 1917; and he also entered the University Officers' Training Corps. He failed Responsions again in June. In fact, he was never to pass it. Except for the fact that Oxford University later exempted ex-servicemen from taking the examination, Jack Lewis would never have been able to stay at Oxford.

It is worth pausing for a moment in this biography of C. S. Lewis, to reflect that one of the most famous incidents in the life of University College occurred in 1811, when it expelled Percy Bysshe Shelley. Why was he expelled? For his part in the publishing of a pamphlet called "The Necessity of Atheism." In it he writes passionately,

> The mind cannot believe the existence of a God. It is also evident that as belief is a passion of the mind, no degree of criminality can be attached to disbelief; they only are reprehensible who willingly neglect to remove the false medium through which the mind views the subject. It is also unnecessary to observe, that the general knowledge of deficiency of such proof cannot be prejudicial to society. Truth has always been found to promote the best interests of mankind—every reflecting mind must allow that there is no proof of the existence of a Deity.

Shelley and his roommate, Thomas Jefferson Hogg, were both expelled from Oxford University, not so much for the content of the pamphlet as for their refusal to come clean about its production. Shelley's subsequent writing, especially the notes of 1813 to his poem "Queen Mab", extols the virtues of the abolition of marriage; its abolition would result in "choice and change," and "exempt[ion] from restraint." He said that prostitution was the legitimate offspring of marriage and its accompanying errors. He spoke of the despotism of marriage. Shelley contended "the vulgar, ever in extremes, became persuaded that the crucifixion of Jesus was a supernatural event." He maintained "the blood shed by the votaries of the God of Mercy and Peace since the establishment of his religion would probably suffice to drown all other sectaries now on the habitable globe." Shelley wrote about the vast distance of the stars from the earth. He explains that in one year light travels 5.422 billion miles, and he speaks of how many years would elapse before light from the nearest star would reach us. "It is impossible to believe," he writes,

> that the Spirit that pervades this infinite machine begat a Son upon the body of a Jewish woman.... All that miserable tale of the

> Devil, and Eve, and an Intercessor, with the childish mummeries of the God of the Jews, is irreconcilable with the knowledge of the stars. The works of His fingers have borne witness against Him.

Shelley was part of a long line of intellectuals, some of them mentioned before in this biography, who were influenced by David Hume and his arguments against the Christian gospel.

The atheistic Ulsterman who enrolled in University College in April 1917 was no mean poet himself. Over the last year he had been writing a collection of short poems entitled *Metrical Meditations,* which was to grow to fifty-two pieces. The day would gloriously come when his pen would run counter to his own and Shelley's atheism, and his robust talent would be given to the service of Jesus Christ. For now, though, the shadow of war fell darkly upon him.

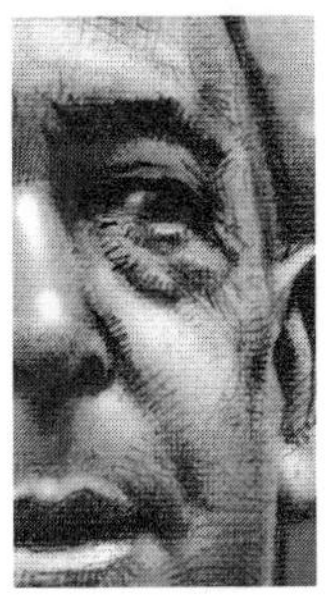

Chapter Nine

IF THERE WERE NO GOD, THERE WOULD BE NO ATHIESTS

The month of May had come. In its past, England has been famous for May Day revels. The first of May became a very important annual landmark. With the long winter over, a maypole was raised on every village green and crowned with garlands. The May Queen was chosen, and games were arranged for the children. There was dancing on the green, and events were open to all. Even town squares and marketplaces had their maypoles.

Children kept up the May festival, even when the maypole became history. They carried garlands of the flowers of May, flowers which they showed at every home, waking late sleepers with their cry:

A bunch of May I have brought you,
And at your door it stands.
It is but a sprout, but it's well put about
By the Lord Almighty's Hand.

The rebirth of nature in May is full of perfumes: lilac in the garden, gorse on the hills, and hawthorn in the valleys and hedgerows. In the forest, bluebells and pines, moss, fern, and tree bark pour out a heady mixture of scent.

It was a Sunday morning in Oxford, May 1917. The towers and ancient pinnacles were gleaming in the sun; daisies and buttercups carpeted the level fields surrounding the city; overhanging trees permitted shade. The flowering bulbs of the Water Walks of Magdalen College were in evidence. Winter aconites and snowdrops had been followed by, amongst others, daffodils, sqills, and bluebells. By Addison's Walk—named after Joseph Addison, the English poet and statesman—the famous *fritillaria meleagris*, commonly known as snake's head fritillary, was flowering.

On this beautiful Sunday morning, some bicycles were abandoned by a swimming hole; animated voices could be heard across its surface. Jack and his friends were enjoying an early morning swim. It was a long way from the emerald Atlantic breakers of County Donegal where Jack had enjoyed swimming in the hot summer of 1916. "Parson's Pleasure" may not have been the white strands of Donegal, but the young student enjoying its refreshing water was now admitting that he had never been so happy.

For Jack these were idyllic days. With his literary temperament, he did not take long to discover the joys of the Oxford Union library, one of the largest lending libraries in the city, and of particular relevance to a student studying classics. The Oxford Union was founded as a debating society, and Jack joined it. Long a forum for high class debating, some of the world's greatest speakers had debated there. The topics for debate ranged from heavyweight political and ethical arguments to more light-hearted options. The forms of debate at the Oxford Union are similar to those of the House of Commons. The debating chamber has no amplification since it was built specifically for debates.

Jack was soon punting with his friends on the Cherwell River. Punting on Oxford's rivers has long been a popular recreational activity. A punt, of course, is a flat-bottomed boat propelled by one person who stands at the rear and pushes the punt along using a pole.

Jack's meals, apart from the main meal of the day, were now served to him in his room at University College by scouts, who were staircase servants. He made friends and talked late into the night with them, more or less overhauling the universe. War's shadow, though, darkened his idyll. In all, there were only 315 students at Oxford University at this time; and Jack was one of only 6 men at University College. Most of the college space was given over to serving as an army hospital.

Jack's stay at University College did not last long. Having now enlisted in the army, he was sent across the city to be billeted at Keeble College, in a carpetless little room with two beds, minus sheets and pillows. He knew he was experiencing only a shadow of the real Oxford. Even when billeted at Keeble, he visited his own college, wandering around it, enjoying its atmosphere, as it stood encased in windows darkened with ivy that had been left uncut since the war had emptied its rooms. Dustsheets covered some of the rooms; others lay undisturbed, as the owners had left them. Jack just loved the place.

Jack's roommate at Keeble was a young Irishman, Edward Francis Courtney Moore. Jack called him Paddy, and they eventually became good friends. In September 1917, on passing an exam, Jack was made Second Lieutenant and was gazetted into the Third Battalion of the Somerset Light Infantry. He was given a month's leave before being posted for active service. Jack decided to accept an invitation from his friend Paddy Moore to stay at his mother's house in Bristol. Jack had gotten to know Paddy's family, who had stayed in rooms close to Keeble to be near to Paddy. Paddy's mother, Mrs. Janie King Moore, was born in Pomeroy in County Tyrone, the eldest child of the Reverend W. J. Askins. She was separated from her husband, Courtney Edward Moore, and had moved to Bristol with Paddy and her daughter Maureen, who was now twelve years old. Mrs. Moore's brother, Robert, was a doctor in Bristol. Maureen later became Lady Dunbar of Hempriggs. Through her father's side of the family, she was heir to the Baronetcy; and she was also heir to an estate in Caithness, Scotland.

Homesick for Ireland, Jack had grown close to the family. It was while at Bristol that Maureen Moore heard a conversation between Jack and Paddy, in which they promised that, if one of them did not survive the war, the other one would look after Jack's father and Paddy's mother. It was a promise that Jack would keep.

Jack spent only the last week of his leave with his father in Belfast. His father was hurt by his action; it led to a division between them, even an estrangement. How Albert Lewis felt is understandable. Jack had spent three weeks with the Moores and only one week with his father, and all in the light of the possibility of Jack's death in battle. Mrs. Moore was to come between them.

In October, Paddy, also a Second Lieutenant, was sent to France with the Rifle Brigade; Jack was sent to a camp near Plymouth. In November Jack sent his father a telegram to say that he had arrived on a forty-eight-hour leave and asked his father if he would come to Bristol where Jack was staying. He would meet his father, he said, at the station. Jack omitted to tell his father that, after his leave, he was to be shipped from Southampton to France. Albert was confused by Jack's telegram. He cannot be blamed for that. He wired his son to tell him that he didn't understand the telegram and asked him to write. As it turned out, the third Somerset Light Infantry was ordered to France after its forty-eight-hour leave. Albert and Jack did not have their meeting. Twelve days after his arrival in France, Jack arrived in the front-line trenches. It was his nineteenth birthday.

In his autobiography *Surprised by Joy* C. S. Lewis does not write of the politics or morality of the First World War. Many questions have been raised about the war: was it avoidable? Was it an error? Did the culture of militarism prepare men so well for war that they yearned for it? Was it Britain's "war of illusions"? Was it maximum slaughter at minimum expense? C. S. Lewis writes more about the people he encountered than about these questions. He writes of a young man in his battalion who influenced him. He was a scholar of Queen's College, Oxford. A highly principled young man, Johnston was moving toward a belief in God. Jack held long arguments with him, about faith in God and a wide range of other topics. It is quite evident that the high moral standards of Johnston pricked Jack's conscience. Johnston, who commanded a company, was killed.

Jack writes with deep irony about his very first entry into a dugout to report to a captain. Blinking in the candlelight, he discovered himself face to face with one of his former schoolmasters.

Jack immediately claimed acquaintance; in response all he got from the captain was an admission in a low and hurried voice that he had once been a schoolmaster. The acquaintance was never mentioned again. Not a kindly word, not an ounce of warmth came from that block of human ice—by such acts are men remembered.

However, Jack notes the kindnesses shown to him by men of higher rank; he rates them much better than the Bloods of Malvern College. Here he mixed with men of all classes and found camaraderie in the midst of the odious and irrational life of the First World War's trenches. He writes with affection regarding two Canadian Officers who, on his very first night in France, treated him like a long-lost friend. Then there was Wallie, the West Country farmer whom Jack reckoned to be the best man in the battalion, and who drew many a laugh for his passionate commitment to the Third Somerset Light Infantry. Any criticism of the Yeomanry brought Wallie's passion to the boil, and he was the butt of many a "wind-up."

Jack highlighted water and weariness as his two chief enemies during that horrendous winter. He went asleep marching and woke up to find himself still marching. Barbed wire pierced his thigh gumboots, and the icy water that filled the trenches above the knee welled up inside his boots. He often came across corpses, and he found that in the midst of life he was in death. He even describes finding men like crushed beetles. Typically, though, not even the misery of the trenches stopped his ferocious reading. He was deep into George Eliot's *The Mill on the Floss.*

In February 1918, Jack went down with what was known as trench fever. This disease is spread among human beings through contact with body lice. The crowded conditions in the trenches, and the circumstances that interfered with the regular washing of clothes, meant that the soldiers were predisposed to the disease. Its symptoms are sudden fever, loss of energy, dizziness, headache, and weight loss. Severe muscle and bone pain can occur; and pain is particularly severe in the shin—thus its nickname "shin-bone fever." The fever can reach 105 degrees Fahrenheit (40.5 degrees Centigrade) and stays high for five to six days at a time. The temperature then drops, staying low for several days, usually recurring in 5-6 day cycles. Untreated, the patient can experience relapses as many as ten years after the first episode. The disease can even cause prolonged disability.

Jack was hospitalised for three weeks at the French coastal resort and seaport of Le Freport, twenty-five kilometers northeast of Dieppe. During the First World War, the port contained three hospitals. One of them was a converted hotel, where the soldiers were placed two in a room. Life is seldom tidy, and Jack's first roommate was a soldier who was having a furious affair with a night nurse. When he was moved after a week, his next roommate was a Yorkshire man who was a misogynist. He suggested to Jack that they should both make up their own beds, in order to keep the nurses out of their room for as long as possible. Ah, such is life!

"Women," said the gifted writer of the book *A Handful of Nations*, "are the only realists; their whole object in life is to put their realism against the extravagant, excessive, and occasionally drunken idealism of men." He also wrote in his book *What's Wrong with the World*, published in 1910, "The Christian ideal has not been tried and found wanting; it has been found difficult and left untried." In his book *Where All Roads Lead*, he wrote, "If there were no God there would be no atheists." Who was this gifted writer? His name was Gilbert Keith Chesterton. Jack lifted a volume of his essays at Le Freport. He knew nothing of Chesterton, or of the fact that he was a prolific and gifted writer in virtually every area of literature. If in the works of George MacDonald he heard the voice of Holiness, lying on his hospital bed in Le Freport reading Chesterton he heard the voice of Goodness. In fact, he said he felt charmed by Goodness through Chesterton's essays.

To my sceptical reader, in the France of 1917 the juxtaposition of the horror of war and the charm of goodness may seem implausible. Yet, as Chesterton put it in 1907, in his *Introduction to the Book of Job*, "the riddles of God are more satisfying than the solutions of man." Later, Jack commented that a young man who wants to remain a sound atheist can't be too careful what he reads. There can be no doubt that, amidst man's bloody and heartless inhumanity to man in the Europe of 1917, the Saviour of Souls was searching for C. S. Lewis.

On 20 February 1918, Jack rejoined his battalion at a village called Fampoux, on the north bank of the Scrape, six kilometers east of Arras. The Battles of Arras in World War I, were five major engagements fought between the Allies and the Central Powers. Jack was in the final engagement, as the Allies faced the final German attack on the Western Front. All day the Germans shells poured into the British lines at the rate of three a minute. Jack even "took" sixty German prisoners, who came out of nowhere with their hands up. Would not shades of the Scottish poet Robert Burns have touched the Irish heart of Jack Lewis when he noted that in the holocaust he, a poor shuddering man, met a poor shuddering mouse, and the mouse made no attempt to get away? It was the poet in him that remembered such detail; and indeed, in the midst of it all, he did keep a notebook, and he did write poems.

Jack was later to pay great tribute to a certain Sergeant Ayres, who aided him as a young officer throughout his wartime experiences. He spoke of how Sergeant Ayres was virtually a father to him. Jack surmised that the same shell that wounded him on Mount Bernenchon killed Ayers. Jack was wounded in his left hand, on his left leg just above the knee, and in his left side just under his armpit, close to his heart. He crawled back and was picked up by a stretcher-bearer.

One sadly imagines one of those "what if" scenarios. What if the fatherly sergeant had lived to see the young Irish officer rise to become one of the best selling and most deeply loved Christian authors in history? What if he'd been able to visit that author at Magdalen College in Oxford? What if he had been able to have afternoon tea amidst the dreaming spires and walk through the local water meadows with C. S. Lewis, in that earthly haven reminiscing about the holocaust they had survived? But it was not to be; the kindly sergeant never saw England again.

The young Irish officer was hospitalised at Etapas. His brother, now Captain Warren Lewis, cycled the fifty long miles from Doullens to see him. Joyfully and thankfully, Warren found him sitting up in bed.

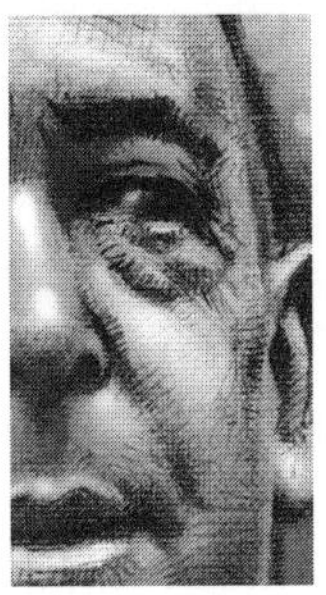

Chapter Ten

HEARTBREAK AT THE HEART OF THINGS

There are six species of deer that can be found wild in the British Isles, but roe deer are the only species that can be considered indigenous. Their summer coat is chestnut-red, although it can vary to a sandy yellow. They can be seen feeding at dawn and dusk. They just love to sunbathe and can be found in sunlit clearings.

The second indigenous deer species in the British Isles is the red deer. The red deer is the largest mammal in Britain and can have a life span of over twenty years. Fights between stags are common and very often cause serious or fatal injury. During the summer, red deer are dark red or brown, with a lighter colour of cream on the underbelly, inner thighs, and rump. Without question, the red deer is Britain's most spectacular mammal.

Fallow deer have a fascinating history in Britain. Norman records mention them; because they were classified "beasts of the forest," they belonged to the king. They can be found today in practically all areas of England and Wales. The summer coat of the common fallow is deep chestnut with white spots.

Another species is the Japanese sika deer. The sika deer was first brought to Ireland about 1860 and put on the Powerscourt Estate near Enniskerry, County Wicklow. In that year Lord Powerscourt bought a stag and three hinds with him from Japan. The sika was then brought to England and exhibited in Regent Park. Due to escapees and deliberate releases, the animal has become widely distributed. The adult's summer coat is bright chestnut and usually includes a row of white spots down either side of the dark dorsal stripe.

The Reeves's Muntjac, or barking deer, the smallest of England's resident deer, is now possibly the most widely distributed in the country. The deer's summer coat is a bright, strong chestnut-red, while the chin, throat, underside of the tail, and region between the hind legs are often white. Recently-cut deciduous forests, with cover of bramble, box, gorse, rhododendron, bamboo, and fern, readily support this versatile deer. They seem to vanish at the height of summer, when the vegetation is thickest.

The least common of Britain's wild deer population is the Chinese water deer. They were first introduced in the 1870's and kept in London Zoo. The majority today can be found residing in close proximity to Woburn Abbey in Bedfordshire, most of them having descended from escapees. It has been suggested that government officials working in Woburn during the Second World War were less than diligent in closing the gates! The summer coat is a rich chestnut to a ginger red. They are considered solitary animals, interacting closely only during the rutting months.

In the warm summer of 1918, Jack Lewis was to be found wandering through bracken in the grounds of Ashton Court, Long Ashton, Bristol, relishing the deer park. At times he found himself coming face to face with a stag, peering at him through branching antlers. After examining Jack, it would snort, kick up its heels, and bound away. Like Gulliver in *Gulliver's Travels,* Jack found more solace with animals than with humans at this time in his life.

Jack was convalescing at Ashton Court, originally a fifteenth century castle. He simply did not fit into the surrounding life of the billiard-playing, noisily shouting, tunelessly whistling young soldiers who were convalescing with him. His recent war experiences caused him to suffer from nightmares that would recur for years. Did he feel at times, perhaps, like the poet Wilfred Gibson?

We who are left, how shall we look again,
Happily on the sun or feel the rain,
Without remembering how they who went
Ungrudgingly, and spent
Their all for us, loved too the sun and rain?

A bird among the rain-wet lilac sings,
But we, how shall we turn to little things,
And listen to the birds and winds and streams
Made holy by their dreams,
Nor feel the heartbreak in the heart of things?[1]

One thing is certain: in the summer of 1918, Jack Lewis was a lonely young man. As an invalid in Endsleigh Palace Hospital in London, he went to Great Bookham to visit The Great Knock. One can only imagine their conversation and wonder how Mr. Kirkpatrick's logic handled the slaughter that was still piling up the dead in France. How did his thinking react to the rendezvous with death at Ypres, Verdun, the Somme, or Arras? The battle of Verdun alone, which lasted from February to December 1916, caused an estimated 700,000 casualties.

When Jack returned from Great Bookham, he wrote to his father about the visit, pleading with him to come and see him. Jack admitted in the letter to being homesick. More importantly, Jack also admitted that he was not always what he should have been in his relationship with his father. From the letter it is obvious that he had a deep desire to see his father and to hold on to as much of his old home life as possible.

Albert resisted what was probably the warmest letter he was ever to receive from his son. This resistance hurt Jack deeply, so it is understandable Mrs. Janie Moore soon filled the gap in his desperately lonely life. She called on him in London while visiting her sister at the War Office. When Jack found it impossible to be sent to a convalescent home in Ireland, he chose to go to Ashton Court in Bristol to be near to her. He still faced the possibility that he might have to return to those long and crowded trenches of France, with their screaming shells and mercilessly raking bullets.

News eventually came of the fate of Jack's friend and Janie's son, Paddy Moore. He had last been seen on 24 March, defending a position against superior numbers of the enemy. After he had been taken prisoner, he had overthrown his guards and got back to his own lines, only to be sent over again. He was wounded in the leg, and as he was being bandaged he was shot through the head and died instantaneously.

Now Jack Lewis and Janie Moore were drawn even closer, and Jack did not forget his promise to look after her. Was he in love with her, infatuated with her? Or was she simply like a second mother? It is a question only he could fully answer.

He was twenty, she was forty-six. He called her Mother, or Minto, and she called him Boysie, and C.S. That she was extremely kind, well read, very hospitable, often autocratic, distinctly anti-Christian, and heartbroken, is indisputable. Now four months into his convalescence, Jack pointed out to his father that his friends were laughingly suggesting that his Irish father was a mythical creation; but still Albert did not go to see his son.

The Irish proverb states, "It's a long road that has no turning." Suddenly, Jack's tortuous road in life turned around what was for him a very pleasant corner. The publisher Heinemann accepted a collection of his poems entitled *Spirits in Bondage*. Jack had been writing the poems since he was fifteen; he shaped together his collection at Ashton Court and then sent it to Heinemann. Jack actually went up to London and met the great Mr. Heinemann himself. Heinemann informed Jack that the novelist John Galsworthy, author of *The Forsythe Saga,* had seen the typescript of Jack's book and wanted to publish one of his poems in his new magazine *Reveille*.

The overall message of his poems is deeply pessimistic, and speaks of a "Lord" who knows no pity and has a diabolical, malevolent nature. If there was a God—and the poet Jack did not believe there was—He was outside the world of humankind and did not care about our world.

Jack's fifty-two poems, written between Easter 1915 and his going up to Oxford in 1917, had been called originally *The Metrical Meditations of a Cod*. Anybody from Ulster will tell you that calling someone a "cod" covers anything from eccentricity to self-deprecation. In truth, it is an affectionate term for behaviour that is endearing, though it may be slightly embarrassing. It seems to me that Jack was doing what a lot of Ulster people do. They know they have a talent, but they try to hide it under a cover of self-deprecation in order to protect themselves from those who do not like "tall poppies." This "poppy" who had emerged from the trenches of France would grow very tall indeed; but it would take a long time before his fellow Ulstermen would appreciate his genius. He wrote *Spirits in Bondage* under the pseudonym Clive Hamilton, admitting he wanted anonymity from officers and men in the army who might criticise him. Jack would have to travel much further down life's road before he would become immune to what the critics thought of him.

A happy outcome of Heinemann's interest in Jack's little book of poems was Albert Lewis's attention to and encouragement in the project. It brought a temporary reconciliation between them. However, after two more moves in his convalescence, one to Perham Down in Hampshire and the other to Eastbourne in Sussex, Jack found he was unable to get leave to go home to Belfast in December 1918. To almost indescribable international relief, the Armistice had been signed in November; but was any kind of truce possible between the often strange and distant father and his deeply hurting son? To Jack's surprise, leave was suddenly granted, and he took the journey home, unannounced. What were his feelings as the Irish shoreline came in sight once more? How did he react in his spirit as he viewed again the Holywood Hills on the portside of the ferry?

As the ship docked at the old familiar port of his school day voyages and he travelled through East Belfast, did Jack wonder how he would be received? As he saw the tower of St. Mark's, Dundela, did he reflect on his atheism? As he came near Campbell College, did he think long thoughts on his past, closer relationship with his father? Across his native Province, tens of thousands of homes had been emptied of the flower of Ulster's manhood. Enlistment in the war had been huge; a multitude of men had "taken the shilling"—an earnest (token), pronounced in Ulster *ern'st*—from Recruitment Sergeants. At Christmas 1918, the enlistment song must have had a ghost-like ring across all the hills of Ireland:

Don't take the shillin' lad;
Don't for heaven's sake.
Don't take the shillin' lad,
Or your mother's heart will break.
You're the only son that's left to me;
Don't let us part.
Don't take the shillin' lad,
Or you'll break your Mother's heart.

Thoughts of his blue-eyed mother must have filled his mind as he entered the familiar gate of Little Lea. The guns of Arras were silent now; the torment of shelling and slaughter were over. It was the morning of 27 December, and he was back in Ireland. Remembrance of the birth of the Prince of Peace had just passed; Jack Lewis, who now called that Prince a pitiless Lord, had come home.

Warren Lewis noted in his diary that day that he, Jack, and his father had lunch and then went for a walk. Warren described the experience as if an evil dream of four years' duration had vanished, and they were back in the year 1913. That evening, the first together in a long time, they had dinner with champagne. As the New Year opened upon a heavily bloodstained Europe, Jack's thoughts turned again to Oxford.

He returned on 13 January 1919 to a University haunted with sadness. Jack attended the first meeting of the Junior Common Room. The minutes were read of the last meeting, held in 1914. There were many empty places. The poet Vera Britten wrote some evocative words that reflect the sadness of the Oxford in which Jack now lived. Vera had achieved the success of getting to Oxford University; but she gave up her longed-for education to become a first-class nurse in the most dreadful conditions. At Etaplas, in 1917, she wrote these words:

> *But still the stars above the camp shine on,*
> *Giving no answer for our sorrow's ease.*[2]

The stars still shone above Oxford; but they still were silent as to why some lives were taken, and some were not.

Jack was now keen to plunge into his academic work and was relishing the beauty of Oxford in that first post-war winter. Together with other ex-soldiers, he was mercifully excused the formerly compulsory Responsions exam, with its dreaded mathematics. He was able to take up again where he had left off, reading Classical Honour Moderations, in which he took a First. This was an examination in Latin and Greek, involving the study of Homer, Virgil, and other great classical writers, poets, orators, and historians. He sat the examination in 1920. He then turned to his final Honours School, usually called "Greats." This was an in-depth study of Greek and Roman civilisation, with a study of Greek or Latin historians and philosophers (including Plato and Aristotle) in the original languages. On top of all this study, Jack was required to study modern philosophy from Descartes onwards. He took a First in *Literae Humaniores* (the name for the whole Arts course) in 1922.

After taking his First, Jack competed by examination for a fellowship at Magdalen College, Oxford. He was unsuccessful. If the disability in his thumbs had led him into writing, this failure led him to take a degree in English Literature and Language, and consequently to write his future significant works in English literary criticism. Truly, failure can lead to our greatest achievements.

In October 1922 Jack entered Oxford Honours School of English Language and Literature, and completed a formidable year of intense studies. He was required to study Anglo-Saxon (Old English), Middle English, and Modern English Philology. He had also to take a paper called Modern English that required a historical knowledge of English from the fifteenth to the twentieth century. He took a First on 4 August 1923.

There are highs and lows through these years of study in Jack's life. The former mentioned rift with his father worsened; Mrs. Moore was at the heart of it. Albert felt that the kind-hearted Jack was being cajoled by the woman's suffering. Janie Moore and her daughter Maureen, whom Jack now regarded as family, moved to 28 Warenford Road, Oxford, to be near him. After a year in college, Jack moved there to live with them. Over the next four years they lived in eight different houses; they were to live in rented houses for eleven years. Albert was jealous of Mrs. Moore's place in his son's life. Jack's visits to Ireland became less frequent; and in July 1919 he had a serious quarrel with his father over money. Warren considered Jack's relationship with Mrs. Moore a mystery. The whole disagreement became ugly, and Jack later viewed his treatment of his father as abominable, and as a sin. The truth is that his father was by no means easy to handle, and that the faults were not all on Jack's side.

However, there were highs, too, in those first years at Oxford. One of them was the beginning of his life-long friendship with Arthur K. H. Jenkin. Arthur, a man from Redruth in Cornwall, was later to become a journalist and a broadcaster. He was to be famous as a writer of books on Cornwall, particularly his one-thousand-page, sixteen-part series *Mines and Miners of Cornwall.*

Arthur was known as "the Voice of the Tinners." Dr. Jenkin, who died in 1980, taught Jack Lewis something extremely precious: how to look away from self, and enjoy a thing for what it is. It was a zest, Jack said, for "the quiddity of things"; i.e., the inherent nature or essence of something or someone. Jack was later to apply this ability to the worship and contemplation of God. To put it simply, we often look up, and then we spoil what we've been enjoying by looking in. Jack explained this error rilliantly, applying it to poetry: he said we make a spectacle of the poet, rather than making him a pair of spectacles.

Jenkin and Jack went for glorious walks and bicycle rides together, enjoying whatever atmosphere offered itself at that particular moment—whether it was a dripping wood, a windy ridge, or a moonlit deer park. If anything was ugly, Jenkin taught Jack to look for its quiddity!

Two more men who became lifelong friends entered Jack's life at this time. The first was Owen Barfield, who went up to Wadham College, Oxford, in 1919. Jack said that his friendship with Owen was like two raindrops joining on a window. They deeply shared their interests together, but Barfield looked at them from a different angle. Night after night they would argue, far into the night. Even as they took walks in the country they would have intellectual dogfights. Lewis always held Barfield in deep affection, even though Barfield was never afraid to interrupt Jack when he was in the full flow of an argument. Barfield always tried to make Jack define what he was saying. Barfield, deeply into the relationship between words and their meaning, was to write many books. Jack was to dedicate his children's book *The Lion, the Witch and the Wardrobe* to Barfield's daughter, Lucy, and *The Voyage of the Dawn Treader* to his son, Geoffrey.

Through Barfield, Jack met his friend Alfred C. Harwood, who had gone up to Christ Church College in the Hilary Term of 1919. Later to become a publisher and marry The Honourable Daphne Olivier, Harwood had an outstanding characteristic: he was implacably imperturbable. He must have been greatly tested in the heated and constantly argumentative world of his immediate friends.

Harwood and Barfield started something special in Jack's life that would bring him some of the happiest hours he ever spent. These were Walking Tours, in which several friends would arrive at a pre-arranged place by train or car and then go walking for several days. They would spend the night in small hotels or village pubs and, after the exhilaration of a long day's walk and before a blazing fire, their animated conversation would range from this world to the next.

Jack deeply enjoyed these times and felt that he did not deserve such pleasure. No doubt, during these golden hours of his life, his thoughts turned to his fellow soldiers of the recent war. Maybe the army chaplain, G. A. Studdert Kennedy, otherwise known as Woodbine Willie, said it best:

There are many kinds of sorrow
In this world of Love and Hate;
But there is no sterner sorrow
Than a soldier's for his mate.[3]

Jack Lewis was to reach grand heights as a writer; but great intellectual though he was, his pleasures were simple. Maybe we ought to call them profound: love of nature, affection for friends, and appreciation of the sheer art of conversation by a roaring fire or on a windy hillside. His walking-friends all preferred to walk on soil that was chalky, because such soil is dry; and they liked the grass to be short under their feet. Arthur Harwood did most of the planning for these walks, and Jack humorously called him "lord of the walks."

Jack also found that good music brought nourishment to his spirit, and he would go to concerts with Maureen Moore or others of his circle of friends. Long after the performance, the thrill of the music stayed with him.

Jack had now obtained three First Class Degrees; he had won the Chancellor's Prize for an English essay; gifted and sympathetic friends surrounded him; but he was also surrounded by poverty. He entered one of the lowest points in his life. He did not have a suitable job, and he began suffering from indigestion, headaches, and panic attacks. In his diary he mentioned, even, that he pondered death. But for his father's generosity, he would have been unable to continue at Oxford. At this time he was passed over for many fellowships.

On his spiritual journey Jack had retreated from any idea of the supernatural and tried to live by good sense. He had also withdrawn from any consideration of the occult and romanticism. This withdrawal was due to his meeting both a tragic Irish parson who had lost his faith and Janie's brother, Dr. Robert Moore, who had lost his mind. At this time, Jack believed that the doctor had lost his mind through flirting with, amongst other things, theosophy, Yoga, spiritualism, and psychoanalysis. Having to hold the doctor to the ground on one occasion was, for Jack, a distinctly frightening experience. The doctor died soon after of a heart attack. Jack turned away from any idea of immortality, and the joy he had known he now looked upon simply as an aesthetic experience. When his friends Barfield and Harwood became followers of the doctrines of Rudolph Steiner and Anthroposophy, he was genuinely shocked. He strongly disagreed with Anthroposophy, the doctrine of immortality, reincarnation, and Karma, seeking to optimise physical and mental health and to place man in union with God.

At this point in the story of C. S. Lewis, I cannot help but think about a story in the Bible. It concerns King Solomon and the Queen of Sheba. "When the Queen of Sheba heard of the fame of Solomon concerning the name of the Lord, she came to test him with hard questions." Solomon was famous across what was then the known world as a hugely wealthy king; yet it was not his wealth that interested the Queen of Sheba. It was his fame "concerning the name of the Lord." Solomon's spirituality and faith fascinated her, and she was obviously sceptical of both. When she arrived in Jerusalem and met him, her questions poured out.

> Solomon answered all her questions; there was nothing so difficult for the king that he could not explain it to her; and when the Queen of Sheba had seen all the wisdom of Solomon, the house that he had built, the food on his table, the seating of his servants, the service of his waiters and their apparel, his cup bearers, and his entry by which he went up to the House of the Lord, there was no more spirit in her. Then she said to the King: "It was a true report which I heard in my own land about your words and your wisdom. However, I did not believe the words until I came and saw with my own eyes: and indeed the half was not told me. Your wisdom and prosperity exceeds the fame of which I heard. Happy are your men and happy are these, your servants who stand continually before you and hear your wisdom! Blessed be the Lord your God, Who delighted in you, setting you on the throne of Israel! Because the Lord has loved Israel forever, therefore, He made you king to do justice and righteousness."[4]

Often, when people are close to conversion, their questions are deepest. What Lewis called "The Great War" was the long dispute he had with Barfield over Anthroposophy. Lewis was arguing from the point of view of atheism, a young man deeply perplexed by many "hard questions." Often, too, the closer people are to conversion, the harder they kick, and the more questions they ask, the closer they are to the answer. This brilliant, ever-arguing, poverty-stricken, deeply confused Ulsterman was closer to the answer than he thought. The *Greater than Solomon* was near.

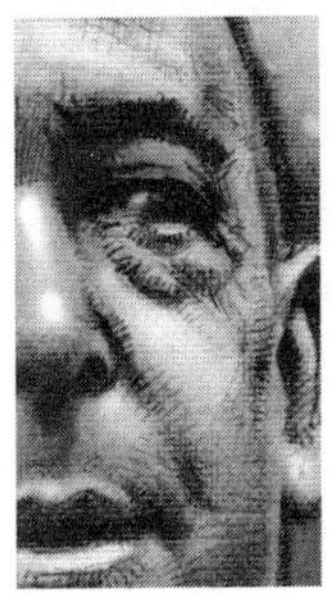

Chapter Eleven

ON FINDING YOU ARE AWAKE

Across England in 1924, May was flourishing in all her glory. The bluebell of England, known before the rose as "the flower of St. George" and worn by the Greeks as a token of remembrance, was blooming in all its loveliness.

Other seasonable plants were in flower; perhaps, next to the bluebell, the most prolific on bank and forest floor was the primrose, with its thread-like stem. The "mayflower" was also flourishing. This was the hawthorn, of course; its beautiful white flower and thorny branches develop small, apple-like fruit that ripen to bright red in the autumn. As a cardiac tonic, hawthorn has been valued since as early as the first century; hawthorn berries have even been called "food for the heart." Hawthorn remains one of the most popularly used botanical medicines for heart conditions throughout Europe. It increases the flow of blood to and from the heart and has also been known to relieve sleeplessness caused by nervous tension.

The most delicate flower in May, with its white, purple-veined, drooping little cup had bloomed on the banks of the forests. It is less well-known than any other spring flower, and it is extremely fragile. It is called the wood sorrel, but in olden times it was called *alleluya.* This is a very appropriate name for the jewel-like flower now joining the rest in praise of the joyous bursting of Maytime across England.

On 20 May 1924, Albert Lewis felt like shouting *alleluya.* A telegram had arrived at Little Lea which read "Elected Fellow Magdalen. Jack." Albert recorded in his diary that he went into his room and burst into tears of joy; and then he knelt down and thanked God with a full heart. In Magdalen Church tower in Oxford, the choir of Magdalen College had sung at dawn on Mayday; and over at University College a full-time job had just been offered to an Ulsterman. It could not have come at a better time for Jack. All he had to live on was his father's allowance of £85 a year and his earnings from grading school examination papers and tutoring one student at University College. It did not amount to much for a man who had to care for a girl at school and her mother.

The Philosophy tutor at University College, Edgar F. Carritt, was going to the University of Michigan for the academic year 1924-25. He was to leave in the autumn, and Jack was asked to deputise for him. Jack's duties were to lecture twice a week for a term of seven weeks, a total of fourteen hours of lecturing. His subject was "The moral good: its place among the values." As far as his audience was concerned, by February 1925 it comprised wo people, one of whom was an extremely garrulous clergyman. Jack brought them to his rooms and allowed them to interrupt him any time they liked. The clergyman virtually took over!

During his year of deputising for E. F. Carritt, Jack applied for all the fellowships in philosophy and English that the Oxford

Colleges were offering. It was to his absolute delight that he was elected a Fellow at Magdalen College, the very last college to which he had applied. His father may have given thanks to God, but Jack was so grateful he said he would have agreed to coach a troop of performing blackbirds in the quadrangle! Though the appointment was initially to be for five years, Jack remained a Fellow of Magdalen for thirty-six years.

It is not easy to capture adequately the history and atmosphere of the college of which Jack had now become an integral part. It was officially founded on 12 June 1458 by William Waynflete, Bishop of Winchester and Lord Chancellor of England. The college has had a long line of royal visitors, including King Edward IV, King Richard III, and the illustrious Queen Elizabeth I. James I tried to make Magdalen into a Roman Catholic seminary, but he conspicuously failed. In October 1642, when Oxford supported King Charles I after the battle of Edgehill, great guns were placed in the college grove, and a battery was set up to defend the river crossings. Magdalen tower was used as a lookout, and large stones were carried to the top of the tower to throw down on any approaching enemy! When the Royalist cause was lost and King Charles, who had made Oxford his capital, had slipped out of the city dressed as a servant, the city surrendered to Parliament. In 1649, Cromwell dined at Magdalen. In more modern times, King Edward VIII, when Prince of Wales, was an undergraduate between 1912 and 1914.

Set against one hundred acres of woodlands, riverside walks, and lawns, Magdalen College has some of the most hauntingly beautiful buildings in Oxford. Standing next to the River Cherwell, the college has an atmosphere of sheer spaciousness. Former students include famous personalities ranging from Dudley Moore to Alfred, Lord Denning; from

Thomas Wolsey to Ivor Novello; from Edward Gibbon to Oscar Wilde. This new Fellow and tutor of June 1925 would become particularly famous concerning the name of the Lord.

We now come to what *The Times Literary Supplement* of 1 October 1955 called "one of the oddest and most decisive end-games he [God] has ever played." C. S. Lewis, in his book *Surprised by Joy,* likened the compulsion of God in his life to the actions of a Divine Chess Player moving in upon him until he was in a position of checkmate. In chess, of course, this is a position of check from which a King cannot escape. This compulsion began in 1922 when Jack entered the English school and began reading English Language and Literature. At this time he made a new friend, a man who came from Skibbereen in County Cork. Nevill H. K. A. Coghill was the son of Sir Egerton Coghill and Elizabeth Somerville, sister of the writer Edith Somerville of *An Irish R.M.* fame. Jack discovered that this tall, broad-shouldered, highly intelligent and well-read man was a Christian who believed in the intervention of God in history.

Jack had been doing his best to outmanoeuvre God; but He was not to be outmanoeuvred. Slowly, ever so slowly, Jack perceived a common trait in the material he was reading. Despite George MacDonald's Christianity, Lewis had been greatly influenced by MacDonald and recognised his brilliance. Jack actually thought the word "Christianity" was not a very convincing name. Instead, he leaned strongly towards the term "Belief of Christianity"; i.e., belief, as against unbelief. He could plainly see that George MacDonald was a believer. As he continued reading, he realised that the books he acknowledged to be of substance, and that had the roughness and density of life in them, were written by such believers. As Lewis put it, they all suffered from religion: Spenser, Milton, Chesterton, Aeschylus, Virgil, even the "religious" Plato—there was something in their writing for the reader to feed on. Others entertained, but were light fayre for the heart and soul.

It is fascinating that Jack picked out Edward Gibbon as one of the writers who were merely entertaining. Gibbon was, as Lewis put it, "tinny." Gibbon had come to Magdalen College as a fifteen-year-old. On 15 October 1764, as he sat musing amidst the ruins of the Capitol in Rome, the idea first arose in his mind to write of the decline and fall of that city and empire. He wrote the book not as an atheist but as a deist. A deist is one who believes the "Divine Clockmaker" wound up his clock but now allows it to work of its own accord; i.e., God created the world and then abandoned it. Gibbon's book became one of the greatest influences in the undermining of Christian faith in the English language. As he traced the first one thousand years of Christianity, and the often-ghastly superstition, wickedness, and folly of professing Christians, he devastated the faith of many. The new tutor of Magdalen College, Jack Lewis, would empathise with Gibbon's belief in an empty, godless universe. But the fact that some professing Christians are hypocrites does not mean that all Christians are hypocrites. Jack admitted that writers like George Bernard Shaw, H. G. Wells, and Voltaire should in theory have been those with whom his deepest sympathy lay; but there was something vital missing in their writing. It seemed to him a strange paradox, summed up in a perversion of Roland's great line in *La Chanson*: "Christians are wrong, but all the rest are bores."[1]

The more Jack read English literature, the more the paradox continued. Further writers like William Langland, John Donne, and Thomas Browne all showed the same characteristic of vitality; but the writer who was really used by God at this time to checkmate Jack Lewis was the clergyman and poet George Herbert (1593-1633). A graduate of Trinity College, Cambridge and Public Orator there from 1620 to 1628, Herbert turned away from worldly ambition to become rector at Bemerton and Fugglestone, not far from Salisbury.

Herbert's writing is private, subjective, and modest. His tone is conversational. Herbert believed that God was revealed in every part of his daily life, even in the humblest drudgery. His style is clear and direct. His message is pure gospel. In his poem "The Sinner," he comes to God as just that:

Yet, Lord, restore thine image, hear my call:
And though my hard heart scarce to thee can groan,
Remember that thou once didst write in stone.

Herbert evocatively described the process of a soul's redemption in his poem *Redemption*. It powerfully expresses, in seventeenth-century English, what Jack was about to experience in facing the God who died in the incarnate person of His Son:

Having been tenant long to a rich Lord,
Not thriving, I resolved to be bold,
And make a suit unto him, to afford
A new small-rented lease, and cancell th' old.

In heaven at his manor I him sought:
They told me there, that he was lately gone
About some land, which he had dearly bought
Long since on earth, to take possession.

I straight return'd, and knowing his great birth,
Sought him accordingly in great resorts;

In cities, theatres, gardens, parks and courts:
At length I heard a ragged noise and mirth

Of theeves and murderers: there I him espied,
Who straight, Your suit is granted, said, and died.

Soon, Jack would realise that the messages and sensations of joy he had experienced were but as the imprint of a wave on the shore, not the wave itself. The desire for joy began to turn to its Object: the images and sensations were only reminders of the living God.

In his second year at Magdalen College, Jack experienced God's compulsion in a most unexpected incident. This time God used a cynic called T. D. Weldon. As God had used an atheist to teach Jack logic, He now used another one to teach him the historicity of the Gospels. As far as Jack was concerned, Harry Weldon was the cynic of all cynics and the toughest of all toughs. Jack reckoned him to be the hardest-boiled atheist he had ever known. One day Harry Weldon and Jack were sitting by the fire in Jack's room, discussing odd events in history. Weldon pointed out that it was strange, but it looked as if the recurring story of a dying god figure in the ancient folklore of many peoples suggests that something of the sort did actually happen. Jack was shattered by this comment; and he moved in for a deeper discussion. However, his guest wanted to change the subject and, as far as Jack knew, he never again showed the slightest interest in Christianity. But the arrow had found its mark: Jack was prompted to look at the evidence, finding to his surprise that it was good. He also re-read the Gospels and could see that they were no made-up stories.

In 1929, in the midst of his busy life at Magdalen College, Jack experienced sorrow at the death of his father. Albert had retired in

1928 in poor health, and Jack spent part of nearly every holiday with him. Stationed in Shanghai, Warren was unable to help.

By August 1929 Albert Lewis was seriously ill, and Jack was to be found at Little Lea, helping his father to eat and shave, and reading to him. There is no record of what he read to Albert, but there was certainly plenty to draw from in that house of books. Here lay the man who did not go to England to see his son before or after he entered the horrors of the First World War trenches; and here was that son now caring for his father and bringing him comfort a few weeks before his death. They had both been deeply hurt by the communication barrier between them. Yet love did find a way through those labyrinthine ways. Jack attested to his father's fortitude and cheerful spirit as he approached death.

After an operation, Albert appeared to be doing much better, and on 22 September 1929 Jack returned to his work at Magdalen. One wonders what they said to each other on parting. Jack had no sooner arrived at Oxford when he was called back to Belfast, arriving on 25 September. He made the familiar journey by train and ferry, and he entered Little Lea to discover that his father had died the previous afternoon. God had been making a powerful approach to Jack; but now the death of his father triggered, or reaffirmed, a belief in life beyond death. The heart knows its reasons.

It is worth noting that the window in St. Marks, Dundela, placed by Jack and Warren to the memory of their parents, reveals the ultimate respect the men had for them both. They honoured them in the end, and that in itself was honourable.

Looking back later on his conversion, C. S. Lewis said that he could see very clearly that he had no more taken the initiative with God, than a mouse took initiative in searching for a cat. He could see, too, that, if Shakespeare wanted to meet his creation Hamlet, the initiative would have to come from Shakespeare. Incarnation would have to be involved.

Consider, then, a double-decker bus going up Headington Hill in Oxford. Visualise the Magdalen College tutor sitting by the window, suddenly becoming conscious that he was holding out against something. He was strangely aware that he was being given a choice. It was not an emotional moment at all, yet he was convinced that if he opened the door that was before him incalculable things would happen. He felt like a melting snowman, or a fox being dislodged from the wood with the hounds just about a field behind him. Those "hounds" included Plato, Dante, MacDonald, Herbert, Barfield, his new friend Tolkien, and another called Dyson. Lo and behold, there was even his sometime-acquaintance, joy!

Did Jack Lewis desire to meet God? He most certainly did not; but God desired to meet Jack Lewis. More than that, He loved him and wanted to transform his life. In the Trinity term of 1929, Jack knelt in prayer and admitted that God was God. Consider that kneeling figure—like Cornelius, the Roman centurion in the early church days, not yet a Christian but seeking God in prayer. Cornelius's prayer "came up for a memorial before God," and God sent the Apostle Peter to help him find Christ. Peter was a Jew who didn't believe that Jews should associate with Gentiles or visit them; and Cornelius was part of the hated occupying power in Israel. God enlightened and changed Peter's attitude; and when Peter met Cornelius Peter spoke of Christ's death and resurrection and how that "everyone who believes in Him receives forgiveness of sins through His Name."[2] As it turned out, God sent help to the formerly atheistic Jack Lewis, brought up in an Ulster Protestant family, in the form of a Roman Catholic friend called J. R. R. Tolkien and an evangelical called H. V. Dyson.

Jack stated that his experience in the Trinity term of 1921 was a conversion to theism, belief in one God. He now started attending his local parish church at Headington, and also attended the college chapel on weekdays. He was not much attracted to church services: he didn't like hymns, and he liked the organ least of all musical instruments. He felt spiritually awkward and inexperienced. He was not the first or the last to feel that many of the local church's perpetual programmes, announcements, and crowds lacked the spirituality of what a "two-or-three" gathering should contain.

He was a believer in God. But he had a great question on his mind. There were a thousand religions across the world; but where had all these things that these religions hinted at been fulfilled? When did one awaken to discover the true and full glory of God? Jack was now convinced of the historicity of the Gospels; but whom did they depict? They depicted not a place, but a Person. Jack came to realise that that Person was lit by a light from beyond this world. Here was the God-Man: God had incarnated Himself in the person of His Son.

Where did Jack come to see this truth? What is more important than when he came to believe in this Person? The answer is that it happened in a motorcycle sidecar, not on the road to Damascus but on the road to Whipsnade Zoo.

What had led to this significant moment in Jack's life? What had brought him to Christ and guided him away from the lands and places he would write of in September 1932? The book he would write during that two-week holiday with Arthur Greeves at Bernagh on Belfast's Circular Road was *The Pilgrims Regress*. It mentioned places as diverse as Claptrap, Haunch, Antinomia,

Woodey, Sodom, Aphroditopolis, Ignorantia, Superbia, Wanhope, and Mania. How did he escape these places?

Before answering these questions, let's go back to the evening of 19 September 1931. Three men were dining at Magdalen College. One of them was Hugo Dyson, who had been introduced to Jack Lewis through Nevill Coghill the year before. Dyson was lecturer and tutor in English at Reading University, and an Oxford Extension Lecturer. He had come to spend a weekend with Jack. The other man was John Ronald Reuel Tolkien. Born in South Africa, he became the Rawlinson and Bosworth Professor of Anglo-Saxon at Oxford. Tolkien and Lewis had become close friends. After dinner, the threesome went for a stroll around Addison's Walk. The walk lies within the grounds of Magdalen College and runs alongside New Buildings northwards between Long Meadow and the Fellows' Garden until it reaches the area called Mesopotamia. The walk that evening was to be no ordinary walk. Its results were to be incalculable. It was going to help lead Jack Lewis to Jesus Christ.

What was Jack's problem with Christianity?

> What I couldn't see was how the life and death of Someone else (whoever he was) two thousand years ago could help us here and now—except in so far as his *example* helped us. And the example business, though true and important, is not Christianity; right in the centre of Christianity, in the Gospels and St. Paul, you keep getting something quite different and very mysterious expressed in those phrases I have so often ridiculed (propitiation, sacrifice, the blood of the Lamb)—expressions which I could only interpret in senses that seemed to me either silly or shocking.[3]

Tolkien and Dyson showed Jack that, if he met the idea of sacrifice, death, and resurrection in a pagan story, he did not mind; indeed he was even moved by it. This was provided he met all these things anywhere but in the Gospels. To put that long, fascinating conversation in a nutshell—Tolkien and Dyson carefully sought to show Jack that the story in the Gospels really happened. Tolkien pointed out that this is a God who is real and whose dying can transform those who believe in him. A gust of wind came through the trees, and leaves fell on Jack's shoulders. But more than leaves fell that evening: spiritual insight fell, too, that was to have wonderful results. They talked until three o'clock in the morning, when Tolkien decided he had better go home to his wife.

Hugo Dyson and Jack continued to walk and talk further. The pair of them strolled up and down the arcades of New Buildings, Dyson urging Jack to believe all that the gospel story presented. Dyson emphasised that, in believing in Christ and His gospel, a person receives peace and forgiveness of sins and can become a new person.

So it was that, three days later, on 22 September 1931, Jack got into the sidecar of his brother Warren's motorcycle, and the pair of them set off for Whipsnade Zoo in London. It was a bright, sunny morning. Jack records that he did not spend the journey deep in thought; he had no inward emotional crisis whatsoever. He confessed that when he got into the sidecar he did not believe that Jesus is the Son of God; when he got out of the sidecar he did.

How did Jack sum up what had happened? He likened the experience to a man lying motionless in bed after a long sleep, being suddenly aware that he is awake. Christ's apostle John put it this way: "We have seen and testify that the Father has sent the

Son as Saviour of the world. Whoever confesses that Jesus is the Son of God, abides in Him, and he in God.…He who believes in the Son of God has the witness in himself.…[A]nd this is the testimony: that God has given us eternal life, and this life is in His Son. He who has the Son has life: he who does not have the Son of God does not have life."[4]

It was a great spiritual transaction that Jack Lewis experienced that morning, and it was to lead him into discovering more and more of the beauty and glory of the person of Jesus Christ. Although the writer of this biography is not seeking to "tidy up" Jack's life (as, for example, some Victorian writers do with their subjects), he does want to point out that what happened on the road to Whipsnade had a profound influence on Jack's thinking. Though Jack continued to have doubts in certain areas, God had begun a tremendous work in him. As he went forward in his Christian experience, God would reveal more and more truth to his heart and mind.

Tracing the writing of C. S. Lewis, we find that he came to see that the gospel fulfils the deepest human aspirations that all other myths are groping toward; and, moreover, that the gospel is true. He came to see Christ as the *Thirst Quencher*, the One who was laid in a stable although He was bigger than the whole world, the One who had, in fact, made it. Powerfully Lewis showed that, considering the things He said, to state that Christ was merely a great moral teacher was ridiculous. Lewis believed that, when Christ died, He died not for humankind but for each human. If there had been only one person, He would have died for that person. He taught that, in following Christ, there were no accidents. He also believed Christ to be sinless, and that His work of ransom on the cross had been planned in Eternity. He believed that His death washed out our sins, and that in dying

He had disabled death. He believed Christ to be the great and final Judge of us all and the King of Kings. Christ, he believed, was the Uncreated Light that drowns darkness. He believed that Christ would come again "as a thief in the night," and that we must be ready for His coming at all moments.

It was a new Jack Lewis that returned to Oxford that September day. The joy he had set so much store by, he came to see, was but a signpost pointing on to the heavenly Jerusalem—to Mount Zion itself. He now stopped striding "the broad way that leads to destruction" and turned to walk "the narrow way that leads to life."[5] But he could not have dreamt of what was about to unfold in his life.

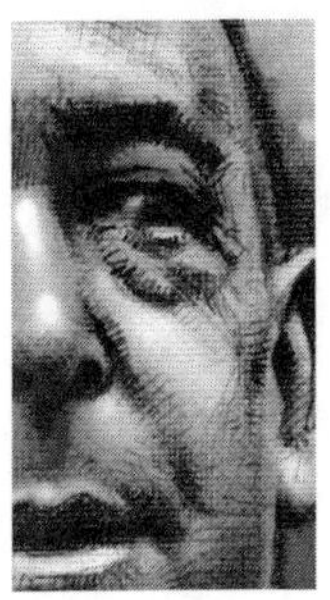

Chapter Twelve

TAKING A HEADER

Some people call December "the dead of the year." Yet, for the careful observer of the English countryside, a few plants are still producing occasional flowers in December. There are the red campion, the hogweed, and the white dead-nettle in the hedges. In the meadows, yarrow and dandelion can be found. In the thickets, crops of shaggy parasol mushrooms come up under the thorn trees.

A careful search in the sheltered hollows of the English countryside in December will reveal the first stirrings of new growth—green shoots poking through the leaf mould, poised to grow and expand when the warmer spring days come.

In the dusk of a December day, an observer lingering in the woods might catch sight of a badger stomping about and grunting. Some people call it the British bear. By the streams, otters come out to fish, and sometimes they cross the meadows to look for another stream. Since their feet are webbed, they are able to move easily on land. High above the valleys and heaths of England, lone kestrels can be seen at times, sinking like stones to capture their prey. The screeching, screaming, and chattering of birds warn that a fox is about. December nights find him on his many nocturnal prowls.

As December 1931 proceeded, berried holly was being harvested to deck millions of homes across Britain. December, with its very own quiet and subtle beauty, its days of sun and wind-scudded clouds in an azure sky, was heralding Christmas. Many children longed for snow; but the small birds loathed the hoarfrost that powdered them as they darted in and out of the bushes; as the hoarfrost penetrates their skin, it slowly melts and chills them to misery. Children, bounding to their windows in the mornings, were fascinated by the frost on the panes. The essayist F. W. Boreham, writing of such mornings in his youth, recalled

> how we stood round [the window], little white-robed shivering groups, and, even while our teeth chattered with the cold, we told each other of all the wonders that we could see in the frozen glass! Such ferns and flowers and forests! Such ogres' castles and fairy palaces! Such ships and seas and desert islands! Such flocks of sheep and packs of wolves and herds of antlered deer! Finding pictures in the frozen window-panes was like finding faces in the glowing embers. There was no end to it.[1]

The village of Headington Quarry lies just about three miles from the centre of Oxford. In Christmas 1931, there were new residents in the area. In October, Jack, Mrs. Moore, and Maureen had moved into their new, permanent, home called The Kilns. Named after the two brick kilns that lay to the left of the house, it was set in an eight-acre garden, half of which was a wooded segment of Shotover Hill. The Kilns lay at the end of a narrow lane that gave it delicious privacy. Jack and Warren had discovered the place in July 1930. It was the stuff of dreams.

Back in April, Jack and Warren had spent their last time together at Little Lea, and they had buried their childhood toys in a box in the garden. They set aside some items to move to England and other things to be sold at auction. They took to Oxford the considerable volume of papers, connected with the Lewis family, that had been kept by their father. Warren eventually typed them up and bound them in eleven volumes that he entitled *Memories of the Lewis Family: 1850-1930.* Today they are on microfilm in the Bodleian Library in Oxford; the originals are in the Marion E. Wade Center in Wheaton College, Illinois.

At the front of The Kilns, there were a lawn and tennis court; at the back a large, beautifully wooded pond, suitable for bathing, lay between the lower and upper parts of the property. The land then rose steeply through little ravines and nooks to a little cliff that was topped by a meadow, ending in a thick belt of fir trees. The view from the top was simply glorious. Mrs. Moore was the nominal owner of The Kilns, with the agreement that, on her death, the house would be left to Jack and Warren for their lifetime. The property would become Maureen's after the death of both brothers. Jack and Warren put up some of the money to purchase the property.

On Christmas Day 1931, the figure of Jack Lewis was to be seen walking the half mile to Holy Trinity Church in Headington Quarry. It was a short journey on foot, but it had been an immensely long journey of mind, heart, and conscience actually to reach that morning.

To understand fully what was going on in Jack's mind that Christmas Day, one would need to read *The Pilgrims Regress.* In the summer of 1930, Jack—who loved to be in water—had been taught to dive by his friend Owen Barfield. Anyone who has known how difficult it is to take a first dive, and how simple it seems afterwards, can empathise with Jack. In *The Pilgrim's Regress* he likens the experience to becoming a public part of the body of Christ. First, Lewis emphasises the necessity of either accepting grace through Christ, or experiencing spiritual death. He then proceeds to what follows on from the acceptance of grace: the experience of becoming a part of the mystical body of Christ and a communicant in the Church. In Lewis's allegory, the pilgrim John stands on the edge of a large pool, being urged to take off the rags he has long worn on his pilgrimage and to dive into the water. Diving simply necessitated letting himself go; as the chapter heading puts it, *Securus Te Projice* (throw yourself away without care).

As Jack walked that half mile to Holy Trinity Church, Headington Quarry, one wonders if he heard the same voices challenging him as the pilgrim John did while he stood on the water's edge. John heard again from people he had met earlier in his pilgrimage; the voices of Mr. Enlightenment, Mr. Media, Mr. Halfway-Sensible, Mr. Humanist, and Mr. Broad tried to stop him from diving in. Judging from the way that Jack writes in *The Pilgrims Regress*, one feels that he did.[2]

In Dickens's novel *A Christmas Carol*, on Christmas Eve Scrooge heard the voices of the Spirits of Christmas Past, Present, and Future; but on Christmas Day 1931 the voices Jack Lewis must have heard were not trying to dissuade him merely from a Victorian-style Christmas of good will and bonhomie. They were determined to distract him from committing himself so publicly to the Christian Church that had been created by the One who was born on the first Christmas Day.

As John "took a header"[3] into the pool (this is distinctly an Ulster expression), so Jack Lewis took his "header," and received communion for the first time since boyhood. He remained a communicant member of Holy Trinity Church for the rest of his life, and was buried in its cemetery. (His Roman Catholic friend George Sayer stated that there is no evidence that Jack ever seriously considered becoming a Roman Catholic.)[4]

What thoughts filled his mind as he headed back to The Kilns? Could he have imagined how God was going to prove to him the truth of Christ's words, "He who loses his life for My sake will find it."[6]

Life at The Kilns now moved along steadily under the careful eyes of Mrs. Moore and Fred Paxford the gardener and handyman. Showing her compassionate side, Mrs. Moore bought a bungalow in sections and had it put up in the grounds of The Kilns, to give a home to an old woman who was in need. The poor and hungry were often fed at Janie's table. Though the daughter of an Anglican clergyman and sister of an Anglican dean, she seriously resented Jack's conversion. Janie Moore blamed God for the death of her son Paddy, and she nagged Jack about his faith. In December 1932, Warren returned from the army and came to live at The Kilns. When he joined Jack for communion at Holy Trinity Church on Sunday mornings, Mrs. Moore chided them for going to "those blood feasts." Her atheism, though, did not stifle her outstanding kindness.

During term time, except at weekends Jack stayed at his Magdalen College rooms. He attended Dean's Prayers at the college chapel each morning at 8.00 a.m. and then went to breakfast in the Common Room. At this time in Jack's life, Common Room breakfast was shared with three men, Paul Beneke, the grandson of the composer Mendelssohn; Professor J. A. Smith, the Waynflete Professor of Moral and Metaphysical Philosophy; and Adam Fox, the Dean of the Divinity School. The ensuing conversations would, no doubt, have made a book in themselves.

Jack usually lunched at The Kilns and had evening dinner "at hall" in Magdalen. Twice a week he would have wine and some fruit and nuts in the Senior Common Room, and he would talk with the extraordinary men who gathered there. His life was full. He tutored students extensively, gave lectures, and did his research during holidays. One result of his early research was his profound work of literary history and criticism, *The Allegory of Love*.

Jack Lewis maintained that Christianity was like seeing the sun. It was not just that he saw the sun, but that by the sun he saw everything else. His conversion to Christ had now given him a fixed point from which to write and teach. He did not try to convert his students; indeed, a student could have listened to him and not known that he was a Christian. The truth is, though, that if a man is in love he cannot hide it; and it would not be long before his love for Christ would be known nationwide. But even as his love for Christ shone undeniably, he wisely did not take undue advantage of his captive audience.

By all accounts, Jack lectured with enthusiasm and aplomb. He had a loud, booming voice, and his lectures lasted for exactly three-quarters of an hour. As his reputation grew, so did the number of students attending his lectures. There he stood, in baggy jacket and trousers, jovially and engagingly giving his views on the literature of the Middle Ages or the Renaissance. He was the only lecturer of the 1930s and 40s to draw and hold large audiences. If he was late for a lecture, he was even known to begin it before he entered the lecture hall. His booming voice would be heard as he came up the steps outside, and he continued lecturing as he headed toward the dais. When he had finished his last sentence, he would step off the dais, hand back the watch he had borrowed from a student, and walk briskly out of the lecture hall, taking no questions.

All great teachers, while they inspire others, need inspiration themselves. While giving out to others, they too need to take in. Jack had undoubted ability as an outstanding literary critic, but he needed those who would challenge and criticise his own writing and nourish his intellect and spirit. These needs were fulfilled each week when he met with the group called The Inklings. Their meetings were for him a truly pleasant experience.

Around 1930 an undergraduate of University College called Tangye Lean founded The Inklings to create the opportunity for dons (university lecturers) and undergraduates to meet together and read unpublished compositions aloud. These works were then discussed and criticised—and maybe even praised. Lean invited Jack and J. R. R. Tolkien, the Bosworth Professor of Anglo-Saxon, to join his club. Lean had two novels published while he was at University and was Editor of the undergraduate magazine *Isis* from 1932 to 1934. Tangye Lean went on to become an extremely talented wartime broadcaster for the BBC. His club dissolved when he left Oxford in June 1933; and that autumn Jack used the name The Inklings to describe the group of friends who met weekly in his rooms at Magdalen.

Tangye Lean's brother, David, became the famous film director of such classics as *The Bridge On The River Kwai, Lawrence of Arabia, A Passage to India,* and, of course, *Ryan's Daughter*. One wonders what kind of classic film David Lean could have produced about The Inklings. Maybe someone, somewhere, will rise up soon and make one. No doubt the camera would pan around the hugely talented characters who met, both on Thursday evenings at Jack's rooms in Magdalen College, and eventually on Tuesday mornings during term time in the back room of The Eagle and Child in Oxford. As those men of learning met to discuss poetry, language, myth, imagination, the state of the world, theology, and, at times, things frivolous, they were an unelected and undetermined group. They had no rules, no officers, and no agenda. The only way in was by invitation. The Scripture says, "As in water face reflects face, so a man's heart reveals the man.[7] A lot of reflection and revelation took place during those discussions.

Above them all it was Jack who loved hearing things being read aloud. It was the poet in him. Here, Professor Tolkien first read his most famous work, *The Lord of The Rings*. He is on record as saying that if it were not for Jack Lewis, he would never have completed the work or offered it for publication. One can imagine the tall, domestic, family-oriented Professor, with his swept-back grey hair, reading his first volume, *The Fellowship of The Ring*. Beginning in 1937, he read it as he was writing it, to that eclectic group of men. Tolkien was not to know that, in the Summer of 2000, when the company producing the trilogy of *The Lord of The Rings* decided to release on its website a short trailer, 1.7 million people downloaded it on the first day! *The Lord of the Rings* has consistently been voted the finest book in English Literature in the last one hundred years. It is certainly one of the most successful books in the history of literature.

Week after week, Tolkien introduced his friends to the story of Bilbo, who during the celebration of his birthday party announced that he was leaving the Shire to see places he had only heard and read about. Soon, Tolkien's friends were hearing of Bilbo's cousin Frodo, who along with three other Hobbits—Merry, Pippin, and Sam—also left the Shire, with the magic ring.

How did The Inklings react, as they heard of the Black Riders of Mordor? What kind of feelings did they have, on hearing of the valley of Rivendell and the Council of Elrond? What counsel did they give to Professor Tolkien? There sat the frail, slight figure of Lord David Cecil, son of the fourth Marquis of Salisbury, one of the best-loved teachers in Oxford University, who had written a life of William Cowper the great evangelical poet. Lord Cecil loved *The Lord of the Rings*. The Inklings were not all enthusiastic about it, however. The comedian of the group was Hugo Dyson, who had played such a prominent part in Jack's conversion. He disliked *The Lord of The Rings*. There, too, sat Charles Williams, lecturer and teacher of St. Hugh's College, whose dominant personality, sadly, was to contribute to an eventual cooling of the great friendship between Tolkien and Lewis. Williams's supernatural thriller *The Place of the Lion* was first published in 1931. The man from Skibbereen, Nevill Coghill, was also an Inkling. Charles Wrenn—who eventually founded the International Conference of University Professors of English, and who helped Tolkien to teach Anglo-Saxon at Oxford—heard, too, of Gandalf, Gollum, and the Orcs. Owen Barfield, with whom Jack was still fighting what he called "The Great War," was also in attendance. Jack's doctor, Robert Harvard, hardly ever missed a meeting.

At their meetings in the late 1930's, no doubt Jack's reading of his own manuscripts caused many an argument. While, Tolkien in *The Lord of the Rings,* headed for the vast upland kingdoms, Jack's imagination took him on spiritual adventures in other planets. His first work of science fiction, *The Silent Planet,* was published in 1938. Here, for the non-Christian reader, he skillfully smuggled theology into his text. Such smuggling was to become very legitimate in Jack's works of fantasy. The evangelist in him was rising. In *The Silent Planet,* he called Satan "The Bent One," and was determined to expose his corrupt ways. Jack's description of Ransom's voyage through space would make even the most uninterested reader want to join him. Jack's lifelong interest in looking at the heavens through a telescope (given to him when he was eleven years of age) had paid off.

There is no question that God had given Jack Lewis a unique and rare gift. He was able to turn Christian doctrine into the language spoken by ordinary people in a way that would draw and hold their attention, and which they could understand. Slowly, he was becoming a very effective Christian apologist. As time progressed, he became an apologist who did not run away from the puzzling elements within Christian doctrine or from that which people found repellent. He faced those elements head on and drew out their great hidden truths for the wide, unbelieving world. He believed the truth of Christianity to be of absolute importance; and he believed that Christ was none other than the Son of God.

The world of Magdalen College looked on with increasing scepticism as their fellow and tutor of English underwent conversion to Christ. Some found it incredible to see Jack heading daily for college chapel. In biblical terminology, it could be said that the newly emerging champion of Christian orthodoxy, while being an Oxonian was *in it, but not of it*. As he pointed out in his preface to *The Pilgrim's Regress*, the Ulsterman who had moved from popular realism, to philosophical idealism, to pantheism, to theism, to Christianity, faced agnosticism everywhere. Thinkers of the day were trying to retain Christian values without Christianity. The writer Virginia Wolff of the Bloomsbury Group described poet T. S. Eliot as "dead to us all," because he had become a believer in God and immortality, and went to church. She believed that "there's something obscene in a living person sitting by the fire and believing in God."[8]

The Inklings, sitting by Jack Lewis's literal and spiritual fire at Magdalen College on Thursday evenings, were proving to be a deep encouragement to him. An inner circle that dominated Magdalen College often looked with a cold eye on Jack's Christian life. Soon millions would gather around the "fire" of this yet unknown Ulsterman and find that their doubts regarding the authenticity of Christ and His teaching were melting. Here was one who would make righteousness uniquely readable and comprehensible, in a nation soon to experience the ravages of another World War.

The Nazis marched into Czechoslovakia on 3 October 1938. On 7 October, many Jews were rounded up in Germany and expelled to Poland. On 28 October, all Jews in Germany were ordered to hand in their passports. By February 1939, England's Home Office announced plans to provide shelters for thousands of households in districts most likely to be bombed. On 3 September 1939, as a result of Germany's invasion of Poland, the British Prime Minster, Neville Chamberlain, declared that Britain was at war with Germany. On 30 October, the horrors of the Nazis' horrendous concentration camps were documented in a massive Government White Paper, saying, "the treatment [of in-mates] is reminiscent of the darkest ages in the history of man."

In November 1939, Tolkien read a section of a new *Hobbit* book to The Inklings, and Charles Williams read a nativity play. Jack read the first chapter of his new book on Christian apologetics, entitled *The Problem of Pain*. As Europe teetered towards war, Jack's book dealt with some formidable subjects: divine omnipotence; divine goodness; human wickedness; the fall of man; human pain; hell; animal pain; and heaven.[9] As the Holocaust descended and a World War loomed, for those troubled by doubts regarding the Christian faith, a sympathetic mind and heart had emerged to affirm the truth of Christian revelation. The old maxim proved itself true: "Cometh the hour, cometh the man."

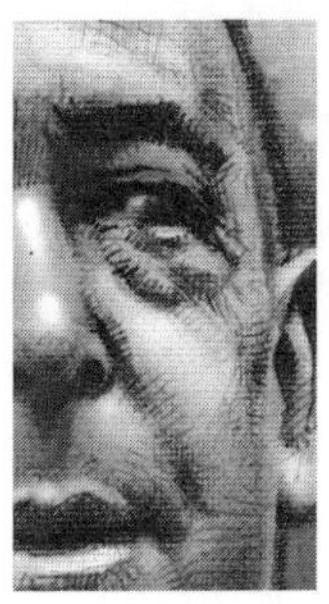

Chapter Thirteen

BEING PRESENT IN THE PRESENT

The trees of England were invaded once more by autumn migrants. Up in the alder boughs, the siskins were flitting and twittering like caged canaries. The gold, fawn, and yellowish-green of their plumes flashed as they hopped from twig to twig, taking from the seed-vessels the food they loved. It was a real change for them from the fir forests of their native Norway and Sweden.

More visitors from Norway heralded the coming of winter: the fieldfares were wheeling in large flocks about the fields. Sometimes, when a whole flock settled upon a thorn tree, they stripped it of an entire crop of haws at one meal!

The beeches of England were in their full glory of gold, russet, and amber. Listening carefully, an observer could have heard the occasional "tchick, tchick" of the great spotted woodpecker as it busily foraged on the bark of an elm tree, tapping away with its powerful beak.

In 1939 the oaks of England remained untouched by the fingers of autumn. The seasonal green of an oak leaf blanches only when there is severe frost and will stay until the turn of the year. The life of the oak is summed up in the foresters' old adage: "Three hundred years to come and grow; three hundred to stand and stay; three hundred to dwine and go."

In *The Peverel Papers* Flora Thompson describes how she once saw a felled oak being hauled through the streets of Oxford. Its bulk was so great and the way so narrow that buses, cars, bicycles, and pedestrians all had to draw aside and wait while the traction engine that drew it negotiated a turning. She mused on how the oak had, perhaps, stood upon some height above the city and "had looked down upon the Oxford of its saplinghood, a castle town with a cluster of mud huts around; had watched spires and domes arise, where before had been green meadows and glinting waterways; and had seen those same spires and domes turn from snowy white to grey antiquity."

Flora mused on how Shakespeare might have halted in the shade of the oak as he rode from Stratford to London; tradition says that he always stopped in his journey at Davenant's hostelry. She wondered if Shelley may have leaned against its trunk on one of his country walks. "Newman," she adds, "may have paced beneath, torn by inward questionings. Who can tell?"[1]

On 22 October 1939, over at the church of St. Mary the Virgin in Oxford, a lot of inward questioning had been going on in the minds of the undergraduates who had gathered to hear Jack Lewis's lecture "Learning in Wartime[2]." He faced head on the issue that they raised: was not the pursuit of learning in wartime like fiddling while Rome burned?

Jack argued that the important point was that Nero was not just fiddling while Rome burned; he was actually fiddling on the edge of Hell. Jack then asked whether it was right for human beings, who were at every moment advancing either to heaven or hell, to be engaged in literature, art, mathematics, or biology at all. To say that it was legitimate in that wider context, but not in wartime, was unreasonable, and giving in to nerves and emotion.

The lecture was one of the most powerful pleas for the legitimacy of learning at any time. Jack argued that there never is a normal time for learning, due to the simple fact that life is never normal. Life is always full of crises and troubles of one kind or another. War does not increase the universal reality of death. Jack was basically arguing that nothing is big enough to be the goal of our existence but God Himself. Absorbing our whole life with a war, giving our whole attention to or living for our country or political party, or class, is giving up what belongs to God alone. So, whether we are a Beethoven or a charwoman, we must get on with our vocation. As the Bible puts it, "whether you eat or drink or whatever you do, do it all for the glory of God."[2]

Lewis argued that, if we get proud to the point that we love knowledge more than we love the thing we know, or grow to delight in our talents more than in exercising them, we must give up scholarly work. We must pluck out our proverbial right eye.

As those undergraduates listened, they must have been comforted by Jack's argument that it is better to leave the future in God's hands, for He is going to maintain it whether we leave it to Him or not. We must never commit our happiness to the future. It is when we work heartily every moment *as to the Lord* that happy work is best done. The Bible states, "Here we have no continuing city, but we seek one to come."[3] Jack argued that if we as pilgrims have been turning this life into a permanent city, war will certainly disillusion us. Humbly offered to God, learning should be an approach, Jack felt, to the divine reality and beauty which we hope to enjoy in the world to come.

Jack Lewis was not a pacifist. He believed that Britain's declaration of war on Germany was the right decision, and that there was no honourable alternative. He believed that the Sermon on the Mount's teaching of "turning the other cheek,"[4] was relevant to daily life, not to war. He maintained that in the New Testament Peter and Paul approved of the magistrates' use of force, when necessary, and he pointed out that the Lord praised the Roman centurion.

Of course, some have taken up extreme positions based on Christ's Sermon on the Mount. Martin Luther gives the illustration of "the crazy saint, who let the lice nibble at him, and refused to kill any of them on account of this text, maintaining that he had to suffer and could not resist evil!"[5] The distinguished novelist Count Leo Tolstoy, on reading the Sermon on the Mount, came to believe that Christ was forbidding the human institution of any law court, arguing that the courts resist evil and even return evil for evil. He argued that the same principle applies to the police and the army.[6]

Jack Lewis was arguing that the duties and functions of the State were quite different from those of the individual. Paul's teaching in Romans 12:17-21 and Romans 13:1-4 certainly bear out his point. The Lord Jesus was not prohibiting the administration of justice; rather, He was forbidding us to take the law into our own hands. "An eye for an eye" was a principle for the law court, not for personal life; Christ was certainly not condoning retaliation.

As a teacher at Oxford, and occupation which was counted as reserved, Jack Lewis was not called up. His brother Warren was, and he served eleven months of active duty, reaching the rank of Major. In May 1940, he took part in the evacuation of the British Expeditionary Force at Dunkirk. Meanwhile, in the midst of all his university duties, Jack spent the first autumn and winter of the war writing his book *The Problem of Pain*. He also joined the Oxford City Home Guard Battalion.

On 14 May 1940, Anthony Eden gave an historic radio broadcast in which he warned of the threat of invasion by means of German parachute regiments. An established fighting force, he said, would need to be in place to see off these unwanted visitors. He urged all male civilians aged seventeen to sixty-five who had, for whatever reason, not been drafted into the services to put themselves forward for the sake of their country. They were to form a new fighting force called the Local Defence Volunteers. By the following day, 250,000 had volunteered; and by the end of the month 750,000 had come forward. By the end of June, the Local Defence Volunteers exceeded 1,400,000 men.

In July 1940, Prime Minister Winston Churchill was responsible for changing the name from the Local Defence Volunteers ("uninspiring," in his opinion) to the Home Guard ("much better," he declared). It became affectionately known as Dad's Army. This new force had to wait some time for proper weapons. While the War Office searched for suitable arms from abroad, the enthusiastic volunteers improvised with rolled umbrellas, broom handles, golf clubs, and all kinds of antique pieces, including blunderbusses, carbines, and cutlasses, which were dusted down for action. In its first summer, the Home Guard eventually received World War I rifles from the United States.

The Home Guard was actually involved in a wide range of activities. For example, the volunteers patrolled waterways such as canals and rivers. On returning from France, Warren Lewis served during the summer months in the Sixth Oxford City Home Guard Battalion on the Thames, in his boat *The Bosphorus*. Other Home Guard duties included manning

Aircraft Batteries—during the war, one thousand were killed while on duty at this type of post—placing obstacles in fields to prevent enemy aircraft from landing, and following air attacks searching through rubble for trapped civilians. They constructed pillar boxes, one of which still stands at the end of Portstewart beach overlooking Jack's boyhood holiday town of Castlerock. They erected defence lines, including anti-tank obstacles and barbed-wire barriers along beaches. One Home Guard Company guarded the Royal Family at Buckingham Palace. The Home Guard practised guerrilla tactics and created special auxiliary units. If an invasion did happen, in the words of Churchill, the Guard was ready to "fight in every street of London and suburbs and devour an invading army."

Any German parachutist, landing in Oxford at 1.30 on a Saturday morning, would have had to face Jack Lewis munching his sandwiches on his way to the Home Guards' meeting place. He would go on patrol with two younger men for three hours, carrying his heavy rifle, much relieved to be allowed to smoke on his tour of duty. He smoked regularly on the veranda of a college cricket pavilion. He was usually back in his bed by 5.00 a.m., on his way home enjoying the dawn rise. He was on duty one night in every nine.

Back at The Kilns, Janie Moore had opened up her home to take in evacuee children from London and other cities. When some schoolgirls arrived, Jack adjusted to the new experience of living with children. He grew to have a great affection for the many children who lived at The Kilns during the war.

Nothing happens by chance, of course. It was the very month that war was declared with Germany when, by making a simple request, one of the children was used by God to plant something in Jack's imagination. The child asked Jack if she could go inside an old wardrobe at The Kilns. She wondered if there was anything behind it.[8] Sixty-five million readers would buy *The Chronicles of Narnia* to find out the answer to her question. Still, it would be almost ten years before the first of *The Chronicles, The Lion, the Witch and the Wardrobe,* would surface.

Many have criticised the narrow confines of Jack Lewis's domestic life, as restricting of his great talents. His friend David Bleakley told me that when he was a mature student at Oriel College he and Jack used to walk out of Oxford to The Kilns of an evening. As an undergraduate, David lived in "digs" nearby. He told me how Janie Moore would sometimes greet Jack at the door, asking him to go to a local shop on some errand or other. David described to me how Jack would get on his bicycle and bring back the potatoes, or some other purchase, in a bag attached to the handlebars. Janie would tell visitors that Jack was as good as an extra maid in the house.

Were all the pressures of domestic life too much for him? There was quite a list of them: a certified "mentally deficient" maid called Margaret; the "hysterical" help, Muriel, who flew into rages; not to mention Warren with his worrying drinking habit. Ultimately Jack was also responsible for the care of the children, who were all over the house and grounds. He had the daily chores of putting up blackout curtains every evening and taking them down the next morning, and, in days of coal rationing, of sawing logs for the fire.

Jack could have lived in his college, but he chose to live amidst all the pressures of The Kilns. Did his decision restrict his talent in the end? The answer is that it didn't; it "grounded" it, making it possible for him to write about how children felt, for example, and about what domestic life entailed. His daily round put weights upon his shoulders; but those weights helped him soar intellectually.

How can weights make someone soar? One day I was talking to a Scottish friend of mine called William MacClachlan. He told me of a boy who was out flying his kite, but he wasn't making a very good job of it. A man came by and gave him some advice. "Put a divot to your draigon, son," he said. ("Draigon" is the Scottish word for a kite; and "divot" is the Scottish word for a piece of turf.) The boy did as he was told, and his kite soared. A bit of "grounding" in our lives will do none of us any harm intellectually. So it was in the life of Jack Lewis. Despite his heavy "grounding," he was about to soar significantly.

One Sunday morning in July 1940, sitting at the Communion Service in Holy Trinity Church, and not feeling very well due to a recent fall, Jack was suddenly struck with an idea. He had been listening to a speech by Hitler the night before on the radio, and to his great surprise he was impressed with how persuasive it had been. He had the idea of writing a series of letters from a senior to a junior devil, giving the psychology of temptation from the Devil's angle. So, *The Screwtape Letters* was born: thirty-one letters about the art of temptation from the elderly Screwtape to the younger Wormwood. Considering the route Jack had passed through on his way to faith, *The Screwtape Letters* was the distilled essence of his journey. Written between July 1940 and February 1941, they were first published in a Church of England weekly called *The Guardian*. In book form, it was reprinted eight times before the end of its first year. As I write, a copy of the Fontana Edition (1968) lies on my desk, and I note that it went through 14 reprints between 1955 and 1968. At least two million copies have been sold. On 24 February 1942, the *Manchester Guardian* reviewer Antifex said prophetically, "The book is sparkling yet truly reverent; in fact a perfect joy, and should become a classic."

The book caused what really became the bane of Jack's life: letters, letters, and more letters. They poured in, and Jack called on Warren to help him. For helping him to handle his routine correspondence he paid him a small salary, and Jack came to lean heavily on Warren's businesslike approach in getting to grips with literally thousands of letters.

In writing *Screwtape Letters* when he did, Jack Lewis shows all of us that some of our greatest work can be done amidst the most appalling circumstances. As Europe descended into the abyss of war, he set his pen to work to show from a most unusual perspective the importance of the choices people make and the reality of the Christian life. The "patient" that Screwtape and Wormwood were working on ultimately slipped through their fingers, because he saw the reality of Christ. In the book Jack shows that the Devil is the opposite of Michael, not of God. He is a fallen angel. And in the last letter Jack powerfully exposes the fact that the Devil is not omniscient: he does not know God's plans or what He is really up to. Jack shows that the "Intelligence Department" of Hell has the greatest curse upon it.

Jack is on record as saying that no writing gave him less enjoyment than did *The Screwtape Letters*. It is little wonder, for he was facing the Devil and his works head on. One wonders if Miss Cowie ever read the book; and, if she did, how did she feel afterwards? Intriguingly, Jack quotes two very famous names at the beginning of the book. They back up his method of defence against Satan in his day and generation. He quotes Luther, who said, "The best way to drive out the Devil, if he will not yield to texts of Scripture, is to jeer and flout him, for he cannot bear scorn." He also quotes Thomas More, who said, "The Devil…the prowde spirite…cannot endure to be mocked." *Resist the devil, and he will flee from you,*[9] wrote James in the Bible. Jack Lewis did just that, and the Devil "ran for it."

Of course, he did not "run for it" everywhere; the evil that stalked Europe was now rattling at the gates of Britain. The Germans were advancing across France and pushing the British Expeditionary Force towards Dunkirk. Invasion seemed to be very close. On Wednesday 5 June 1940, a service of intercession and prayer was held at Westminster Abbey. Churchill, who was in attendance, recalled afterwards, "The English are loathe to expose their feelings; but in my stall in the choir I did feel the pent-up passionate emotion and also the fear of the congregation, not of death or wounds or material loss, but of defeat and the final ruin of Britain."[10]

Thirteen days later, in one of his greatest speeches, Churchill expressed what he felt to be the extent of the threat of the evil facing Britain and the world. On 18 June, the Prime Minister went on air on the BBC to vow that England would continue the battle alone. The day before, the French leader Petain had sued for peace, and Churchill wanted to discount any such speculation. His were awesome words in the face of unmitigated evil:

> Upon this battle depends the survival of Christian civilisation. Upon it depends our own British life, and the long continuity of our institutions and our Empire....Hitler knows that he will have to break us on this island or lose the war. If we can stand up to him all Europe may be free and the life of the world may move forward into broad, sunlit uplands. But if we fail, then the whole world, including the United States, including all we have known and cared for, will sink into the abyss of a new Dark Age made more sinister, and perhaps more protracted, by the lights of perverted science. Let us therefore brace ourselves to our duties, and so bear ourselves that if the British Empire and its Commonwealth last for a thousand years, men will still say: "*This* was their finest hour."[11]

The Director of Religious Broadcasting at the BBC in those momentous days was the Reverend James Welch. He faced the biggest challenge of his working life. To this day, anyone passing through the swing doors of Broadcasting House in London's Portland Place has only to look up to see fascinating words, inscribed in Latin in gold letters, on the walls. Translated, they read: "This temple of the arts and muses is dedicated to Almighty God by the first Governors of Broadcasting in the year 1931, Sir John Wreath being Director-General. It is their prayer that good seed sown may bring forth a harvest and that the people, inclining their ear to whatsoever things are beautiful, and honest, and of good report, may tread the path of wisdom and uprightness." These words, of course, are inspired by Paul's words in Philippians 4:8. At the back of the entrance hall is a sculpture of The Sower; and below it is the Latin inscription meaning "God gives the increase." The Reverend Welch was a sower; and his field was strewn with the horrors of war.

In April 1940, James Welch had gone on a five-day tour of the British Expeditionary Force in France, asking the young soldiers what they thought of the BBC broadcasts. He discovered that the BBC was falling short of their expectations. Welch considered that the listeners in Britain fell into three broad categories: those who approved of religious broadcasting, those who were indifferent but not unfriendly towards it, and those who were overtly hostile. Welch reckoned that two-thirds lived without any reference to God, and that religious broadcasts were of little everyday relevance to them. There was a widespread ignorance of the Christian faith, yet there was a disaffection of materialism and a leaning towards a spiritual interpretation of life. Even among the two-thirds unresponsive or hostile to Christianity, Welch recognised "an almost unanimous consensus of opinion that in the Man Jesus lay the key to many of the riddles of life."[12]

The propaganda threat from Germany was significant. James Joyce, known as Lord Haw-Haw, was drawing an audience of six million a night. After the main BBC News Bulletin at 9.00 each evening, the British retuned their radios to listen to Joyce's mixture of propaganda and boastfulness, prefixed by his chilling introduction, "Germany calling, Germany calling." In an attempt to draw them away from Joyce's poison, the BBC responded with one of its most famous wartime programmes, called *Post Script.*

How, then, was religious broadcasting to respond to the challenge of addressing a nation at its time of deepest need? In September 1940, London was facing the blitz. By the end of the month, 7,000 people had been killed and 9,000 injured. Welch needed a voice that would have a novel approach to religious broadcasting. In such dire times, who could deal with the doubts that people were having? Recently, Welch had been reading a book called *The Problem of Pain* by C. S. Lewis. He recognised that he had discovered a refreshingly innovative mind and a rare gift. The book that Jack had penned between the summer of 1939 and the spring of 1940 had deeply touched the mind and heart of the man who wrote these words:

> In a time of uncertainty and questioning it is the responsibility of the church—and of religious broadcasting as one of its most powerful voices, to declare the truth about God and His relation to man. It has to expound the Christian faith in terms that can be easily understood by ordinary men and women and to examine the ways in which that faith can be applied to present-day society during these difficult times.[13]

On 7 February 1941, Welch sat down and wrote to Jack at Magdalen College. Although Welch's mind and heart were very much in the present, the repercussions of his letter were to reach into Eternity.

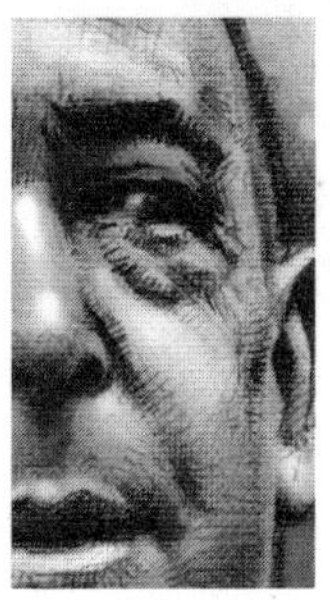

Chapter Fourteen

A CLUE TO THE MEANING OF THE UNIVERSE?

August was rich with wild fruits in the England of 1941. The slender rowan trees were bending beneath the heavy clusters of their orange berries that were now beginning to deepen in colour to scarlet. Hips and haws were plentiful, and even the holly berries, though green, were in abundance. Early blackberries were ripening. The thistle thickets were full, and the goldfinch was to be seen pulling at the thistledown.

The hedgerows, also, were blazing that summer with the hawkweed family, including tansy and ragwort. Here, there, and yonder, were patches of lady-glove and sunflowers growing tall. Nasturtiums were overflowing from cottage gardens onto the roadside banks. Acres of purple heather were blooming, and the cornfields painted the countryside in gold. Bees were busy on the heath, collecting nectar known as heather-honey.

The flowers of high summer were everywhere: common bird's-foot trefoil, fleabane, purple loosestrife, great knapweed, red bartsia, the tall and handsome nettle-leaved bellflower, meadowsweet, and yarrow. Butterflies were busy, including the small tortoiseshell and the holly blue; and on leafy tree and hedge the beautiful seven-spot ladybird beetle could be easily identified. Here, then, were acres of abundant goodness.

In the depths of the countryside, it would have been hard to believe that a nation was fighting for its very life. Back on 10 May, in brilliant moonlight, 550 German planes had indiscriminately dropped hundreds of high-explosive bombs, and one hundred thousand incendiaries within a few hours. The Chamber of the House of Commons had been reduced to a heap of rubble, and the square tower of Westminster Abbey had fallen in. Over recent months of bombing, the casualty toll in London had reached 20,000 killed and 25,000 badly injured; for the first time, people were seen weeping openly in the streets in despair.

On Wednesday 6 August, a train pulled into Paddington Station. The station had itself suffered from German bombing. The train carried Jack Lewis on his way to make his first broadcast for the BBC's Religious Broadcasting Department. James Welch had managed to persuade Jack to come and give his first live broadcast from the London studios. It was billed as follows in the *Radio Times*:

> 7.30 p.m. News in Norwegian
> 7.45 p.m. "Right and Wrong"
> A clue to the meaning of the universe?[1]

His first broadcast was squeezed between the nightly news in Norwegian and songs from the National Eisteddfod of Wales.

It was hardly prime time, but the nation suddenly discovered a prime mind on its airwaves, communicating with an extraordinarily captivating voice. Here was a speaker who had passion and enthusiasm, and who spoke with irresistible logic and clarity. People all over the country pricked up their ears, wondered who the speaker was, and found themselves using parts of their brains they hadn't used for years. By the end of the fourth fifteen-minute talk that Jack gave every Wednesday evening during August 1941, letters had poured into the BBC. This broadcaster, by the hand of God, was causing spiritual waves. His second talk, on 13 August, was entitled "Scientific Law and Moral Law", his third, on 20 August, "Materialism or Religion?" and his fourth, on 27 August, "What Can We Do About It?" He also broadcast on 6 September, under the title *Answers to Listeners*.

In Bible times, in the face of the approaching genocide of the Jewish people in the Persian Empire, it was Mordecai who challenged Queen Esther: had she "come to the Kingdom for a time such as this"?[2] So it was with C. S. Lewis: the spiritual life of Britain was facing the arid desert of Nazism and its godless tenets. James Welch and Lewis's producer, the Reverend Eric Fenn, Assistant Director of Religion at the BBC, did a sterling job in preparing Jack to face the microphone. Once there, it was the lessons learned from the many years of his spiritual journey that spilled out like spiritual nectar.

Back in Oxford in those momentous times, the spiritual nectar of Jack's life was spilling out in another very influential corner. In 1928, standing on the banks of a South African river, a twenty-one-year-old girl called Elia Estelle Aldwinckle, otherwise known as Stella, had decided to give her life to helping people find God. Her spiritual journey had led her to Oxford. She had joined the Oxford Pastorate attached to St. Aldate's Anglican Church. She became Chaplain to Women Students and was sent to Somerville College, a women's college, to act as an advisor there.

Stella was a Christian with vision and stamina and an intellect brimming with vitality. Led by God to a vital ministry, she rose up to fulfil it. Not waiting for undergraduates to come to church services to hear the gospel, she took the gospel to them. One day Stella was faced with a challenge. A student at Somerville College complained that she could find no one ready to discuss the questions which agnostics raised about God. Stella decided to do something about it. In the Michaelmas Term of 1941 she pinned up a notice, encouraging "all atheists, agnostics, and those who are disillusioned about religion, or think they are" to meet in the Junior Common Room. The result of the meeting was the founding of the Oxford University Socratic Club in December 1941.

Socrates was the ancient Greek philosopher who never wrote a book. His life and ideas were recorded by his pupil, the great philosopher Plato, and the historian Xenophon. Socrates liked to spend his time in the streets and marketplaces of Athens talking to whoever would listen to him. He exhorted his listeners to "follow the argument, wherever it led them." Stella founded her club "to apply Socrates" principle to one particular subject matter: the *pros* and *cons* of the Christian Religion."

The Club was to continue for thirty-one years. It met every week on Monday evenings during term time, and C. S. Lewis was its first President. At each meeting, a believer or a non-believer would read a paper. A speaker who held the opposing view would reply, and the meeting was then thrown open for a general discussion. During Jack's time it became one of the best-attended and best-known societies in Oxford University. Many undergraduates looked back fondly to their Monday evenings at the Socratic Club. It became a highlight of their days at Oxford. Many a principle expounded there in defence of the Christian faith proved to be so useful to young people struggling intellectually with their faith; these principles strengthened and nourished them in an environment full of scepticism and indifference. Jack, the blossoming Christian apologist, was busy; and his feet were steadily carrying him to declare the Good News even in the form of rigid intellectual debate.

God had even more for His servant to do. One rainy evening in the winter of 1941, two clergymen visited Magdalen College to seek Jack's help. One was the Reverend Maurice Edwards, Chaplain-in-Chief of the Royal Air Force, and the other was the Reverend Charles Gilmore, his assistant. They asked Jack if he would give talks on theology to the men and women of the Royal Air Force. He would be in an honorary role as a visiting lecturer, and the lectures would take place in the many training establishments and camps across the United Kingdom. The idea had come from the Dean of St. Paul's Cathedral, no less. Jack agreed to the lectureship, and so began a ministry to the RAF which was to last for several years. Who can measure the worth of what he accomplished?

Jack was usually away for two or three days at a time, travelling through England, Scotland, and Wales, seeking to win RAF personnel for Christ. The year 1941 was the date of the introduction of the Lancaster, possibly the most famous RAF bomber of all time. In January, the RAF began attacks on specific targets in France. In February, the RAF made attacks on oil depots in Rotterdam and German naval targets in Brest harbour. During February and March, Bomber Command began regular nighttime bombing of industrial targets in Germany. These attacks normally included around one hundred aircraft. In May, the German battleship *Bismarck* was spotted by the RAF, as the ship attempted to reach Brest for repairs. This led to her final defeat by a Royal Navy battle group. In June, the RAF Coastal Command was formed in Northern Ireland, with American-built Liberator patrol aircraft.

Through the opening months of 1941, Jack Lewis was visiting RAF establishments where people were experiencing grief at losing pilots killed in the theatre of war or missing in action. He was talking to men who could be scrambled into an air attack at any minute and who could be dead within hours. By February 1943, a round-the-clock Allied strategic bombing campaign had begun in Europe; in two days, 26 and 27 February, more than two thousand sorties were flown against enemy targets. On 16 and 17 May, the RAF Dambusters breached the Mohne and Eder Dams in the industrial heart of Germany, with a loss of fifty-three aircrew. A raid in July on Hamburg led to forty thousand deaths.

In his Christian witness to the RAF, Jack found the main hurdle to be overcome was this: his audience felt that God was in the dock, and that man had become His judge on the bench. Jack reckoned that the average RAF person, and most unbelievers in his time, would be ready to listen to God's defence for permitting war, poverty, and disease. Some Jewish people, understandably, felt the same. Several Jewish authors have told the story of how one afternoon in a sub-camp of Buchenwald, "a group of learned Jews decided to put God on trial for neglecting His chosen people. Witnesses were produced for both the prosecution and defence; but the case for the prosecution was overwhelming. The judges were Rabbis. They found the accused guilty and solemnly condemned Him."[3]

In recent years, too, many horrors have been witnessed, from the Killing Fields of Cambodia, to the slaughter in Rwanda, to the attacks of September 11th 2001 in New York and Washington D.C., to the grief of Sudan. Does Christianity have any answer to suffering? Consider the following playlet called *The Long Silence*. It is worth meditating upon:

> At the end of time, billions of people were scattered on a great plain before God's throne.
>
> Most shrank from the brilliant light before them. But some groups near the front talked heatedly—not with cringing shame, but with belligerence.
>
> "Can God judge us? How can He know about suffering?" snapped a pert young brunette. She ripped open a sleeve to reveal a tattoo number from a Nazi Concentration Camp. "We endured terror, beatings, torture, death!"
>
> In another group, a Negro boy lowered his collar. "What about this?" he demanded, showing an ugly rope burn. "Lynched, for no crime but being black!"
>
> In another crowd stood a pregnant schoolgirl with sullen eyes. "Why should I suffer?" she murmured. "It wasn't my fault."
>
> Far out across the plain there were hundreds of such groups. Each had a complaint against God for the evil and suffering that He permitted in His world. How lucky God was to live in heaven where all was sweetness and light, where there was no weeping or fear, no hunger or hatred! What did God know of all that man had been forced to endure in this world? "God leads a pretty sheltered life," they said.

So, each of these groups sent forth their leader, chosen because he had suffered the most—a Jew, a Negro, a person from Hiroshima, a horribly deformed arthritic, a thalidomide child. In the centre of the plain, they consulted with each other. At last, they were ready to present their case. It was rather clever. Before God could be qualified to be their judge, He must endure what they had endured.

Their decision was that God should be sentenced to life on earth—as a man! "Let Him be born a Jew. Let the legitimacy of His birth be doubted. Give Him work so difficult that even His family will think Him out of His mind when He tries to do it. Let Him be betrayed by His closest friends. Let Him face false charges, be tried by a prejudiced jury and convicted by a cowardly judge. Let Him be tortured.

At the last, let Him see what it means to be terribly alone. Then let Him die. Let Him die so that there could be no doubt that He died. Let there be a great host of witnesses to verify it."

As each leader announced his portion of the sentence, loud murmurs of approval went up from the throng of people assembled.

And when the last one had finished pronouncing sentence, there was a long silence. No one uttered another word. No one moved. For, suddenly, all knew that God had already served His sentence.[4]

The eleventh of January 1942 found Jack back in London on the BBC, beginning a new weekly series of talks under the title "What Christians Believe." Each was transmitted on the BBC Home Service from 4.45 to 5.00 p.m. The talks were awesome in logic and content. Justin Phillips, in his insightful book *C. S. Lewis at the BBC* comments on the four talks. He says that, in just four talks, Lewis had "moved from the arguments against atheism and pantheism and schoolboy religion, to the inescapable reality of God and of good and evil." He points out that Jack "confronts the listener with the stark choice of coming to terms with who Jesus is—a lunatic, a fiend, or, what He claims, God Himself; and he explains the significance of Christ's death and our proper response of repentance and faith."[5] A third series of eight talks on Christian behaviour went out on the Forces' network on Sunday afternoons from 2.50 to 3.00 p.m. between 20 September and 8 November 1942. Jack's BBC talks were eventually brought together in his book *Mere Christianity*. "Its success is not just because of Lewis's unique skill as a communicator," commented Phillips in 1999, "but because of the person he writes about. Christianity without Christ is just another dogma. "Mere Christianity" with Christ at its heart, remains C. S. Lewis's most important contribution to contemporary thought."[6]

The output from Jack during the war years was a perfect example of Christ's statement, if anyone drinks of the water He gives, it will become "in him a fountain of water springing up into everlasting life."[7] The metaphor is apt. Between 1942 and 1946, the books just flowed and flowed. In 1943 *A Preface to Paradise Lost* was published. It is now one of the most widely read books on the poem. Milton remained one of Jack's favourite poets. In his book, Jack identifies with Milton's emphasis on the virtue of chastity and his opposition to the deadly sin of pride; he emphasises, too, how it is vital to be subservient to God. Jack was showing the relevance of Milton's epic poem to the modern day. He had first read it when he was only nine years of age.

In April 1943 came *Perelandra*, a powerful space novel influenced by the question, "What would have happened if Adam had scolded or chastised Eve and interceded with God on her behalf?" The book is about carrying out what God intends.

In February 1943, Jack gave the Riddell Memorial Lectures at Durham University, lectures entitled "The Abolition of Man: Reflections on Education with Special Reference to the Teaching of English in the Upper Forms of Schools." It was a formidable defence of such traditional values as duty, kindness, justice, mercy, and love. It was also a cutting-edge attack on any science that rejected traditional values. Jack was warning that man's conquest of nature could lead to the actual abolition of the human race. As human cloning already comes ever nearer, Jack's warnings are even more relevant in the twenty-first century. The thought of genetics in the wrong hands is horrendous. Of course, Christ taught that in the end, if it were not for His coming intervention, the human race would be wiped out.[8]

In 1945 *That Hideous Strength* appeared, a book which had been completed in 1943. Here Jack rises to bring a frontal attack on scientific materialism. *That Hideous Strength* presents shades of the Tower of Babel,[9] called in the book, "The National Institute of Co-ordinated Experiments."[10] The book is about an elitist inner circle taking charge and seeking to bring about what they think is good for others, involving sterilisation of the unfit, selective breeding, liquidation of backward races, pre-natal education, vivisection, biochemical conditioning of the brain, and the eventual elimination of organic life.

In 1943, at the suggestion of the American writer Dorothy L. Sayers, Jack started writing a book on the subject of miracles, which was published in 1947. What is particularly intriguing in this work is its attack on the long and corrosive arguments of

David Hume on the authenticity of the Christian faith. Hume's influence in undermining Christianity in Britain has already been traced in this biography; but it is important to point out that Jack Lewis, in his days as an atheist, was deeply influenced by Hume's *Essay on Miracles* (1748). In Chapter 14 of *Miracles: A Preliminary Study*, dealing with the Incarnation, Jack went for Hume's arguments with a passion. He argues that every other miracle prepares for the Incarnation, exhibits it, and results from it. Hume argued that the more often a thing has been known to happen, the more probable it is that it should happen again; the less often, the less probable. He argued that we should judge the probability of miracles by our "innate sense of the fitness of things." So, by Hume's standards, since the Incarnation has happened only once, it is infinitely improbable. So should we dismiss it? Jack lifts his pen, but it becomes an unsheathed sword in the defence of the great story of redemption. He argues that the history of the earth has happened only once; does that make it improbable? Does the Incarnation meet the standards of our "innate sense of the fitness of things"? Jack asks that if someone brings along a newly discovered part of a novel or a symphony, the best way to work out its authenticity would be to see if it fits into the whole, if it illuminates all the other parts and pulls them together. Its own comprehensibility is far less important than its ability to illuminate and integrate the rest.

As he read Jack's defence of the Incarnation, this biographer felt a shiver of wonder in his mind and heart. It is, in truth, exceptionally beautiful writing. Here, Jack points out that all our righteousness is filthy rags. Here, he expounds the vicarious nature of Christ's Incarnation, the sinless Man suffering for the sinful. And he highlights Christ's mind-boggling stoop in order to lift us up. Jack goes on in his book to show that the Baby of Bethlehem grew to meet, fight, and beat the King of Death. He expounds the truth of the authenticity of the Resurrection, and points to the true wealth that lies ahead in the New Creation. He likens it to swapping the ponies given to us in childhood for greater mounts, even now perhaps snorting and pawing in the king's stables, expecting us. A. C. Scupholme put it perfectly when he said of the author of *Miracles,* "the rare combination of the gifts of poet, philosopher, and theologian is quite irresistible."[11]

Slowly, ever so slowly, the Second World War was coming to an end. The lights were beginning to come on again in Oxford, and an increasing number of windows were being unblackened. By April 1945, the Allies were in Berlin. Hitler, deep in his bunker, shot himself on the afternoon of April thirtieth. The Austrian boy who had earned a few shillings painting picture postcards had gone on to cause the death of some thirty million people in Europe. On 7 May, in a small red schoolhouse in Rheims, the Germans signed the Instrument of Unconditional Surrender. The drabness and privation of five years of war gave way to scenes of unrestrained joy across Britain, including the streets of Oxford.

Jack was deeply grateful for having been spared; yet victory in war was followed by a time of great personal grief. On 10 May, his friend Charles Williams was suddenly seized with pain. He underwent operation at the Radcliff Infirmary. On 15 May, Jack went to the Infirmary to see his friend, taking with him a book he wished to lend him, only to be told when he got there that Williams had died. Jack went immediately to a meeting of The Inklings, taking place a few minutes away from the Infirmary, and told the others of the sad news. He later spoke of how the very streets looked different, and how he had some difficulty in making his friends understand what had happened. There is no question that, during the war years, Charles Williams was Jack's closest friend. He had discussed all his books with Jack, and had been a great encouragement to him. In turn, Jack recognised Williams's poetic gift. He was intrigued with the fact that Williams's face, generally considered ugly, became like the face of an angel when he spoke, and Jack loved his open spirit. Later in life, when faced with problems, Jack would muse on "what Charles Williams would have done." It was a lasting measure of what Jack thought of him.

Jack now set his mind and heart back in his work at Oxford, turning away from constant pleadings from the BBC to broadcast. The BBC did everything in its power to get him back to the microphone, but only with limited success. He had moved on, and after his three sets of wartime talks he did no other theological series. His choice was a wise one, because books last longer than broadcasts. Marshall McCluan, the futurist, once wrote that the written word is obsolete. The only problem is that he had to write a book to say so, and fifteen in all to prove it! Millions of us have lived to be glad that C. S. Lewis chose to concentrate on books rather than on the microphone.

Jack's unique work as a broadcaster, though, did not go unrecognised in academia. On 28 June 1946, Jack travelled by rail with Warren into Fife in Scotland to the ancient University of St. Andrews, where he was made a Doctor of Divinity. At the degree ceremony Jack's promoter, Professor D. M. Bailley, the Dean of the Faculty of Divinity, said these words:

> With his pen and with his voice on the radio Mr. Lewis has succeeded in capturing the attention of many who will not readily listen to professional theologians, and has taught them many lessons concerning the deep things of God. For such an achievement, which could only be compassed by a

> rare combination of literary fancy and religious insight, every Faculty of Divinity must be grateful. In recent years Mr. Lewis has arranged a new kind of marriage between theological reflection and poetic imagination, and this fruitful union is now producing works which are difficult to classify in any literary genre: it can only be said in respectful admiration that he pursues "things unattempted yet in prose or rhyme." It is not very frequently that the University confers its Doctorate of Divinity upon a lay theologian, but it may well be proud to give this acknowledgement to the work of C. S. Lewis.[12]

The new Doctor of Divinity was about to surprise the world by turning to communicate with a very different audience. He was about to begin his most influential work, because through the mind of a child the world is reached.

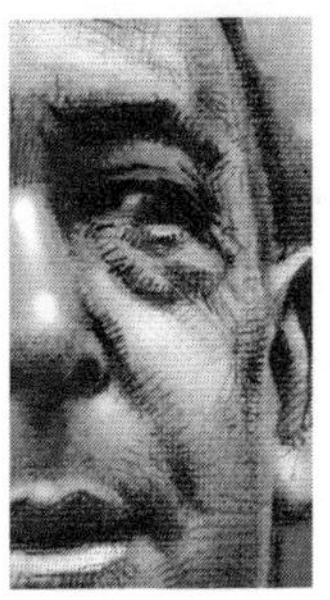

Chapter Fifteen

STRANGE AND SOLEMN PERFUME

> Light changes constantly in the Mournes as clouds bowl their shadows over the rough hillsides and the solid white farmhouses in rushy valleys. Pass in the morning and the fresh whitewash is almost too bright to look at; a minute later everything can be in cold shadow. Hours later it certainly will be. Further up, above the cornfield line, above the sheep-cropped grass you can sit in perfect solitude on a dry-stone wall warmed in the sun. A slight wind sings through the stone tracery, a grasshopper cheeps, a lark spirals, a hawk hunts. Listen harder, for a stream trickles.[1]

So writes Ian Hill about Mourne Country in County Down. At the foothills of the Mourne Mountains lies the former estate of the Earls of Roden. It is called Tollymore Forest Park, and it is truly one of the most delightful places in Ireland.

Here flows the now quiet, now cascading Spinkwee River, and on nearby Foley's bridge an inscription reads thus:

Here, in full light, the russet plains extend,
There, wrapped in clouds, the bluish hills ascend,
Even the wild heath displays her purple dyes,
And 'midst the desert, fruitful fields arise.

It is not the only inscription in Tollymore Park. On a standing stone, another inscription bids the traveller to "stop, look around and praise the name of Him who made it all." I reckon Jack Lewis would have stopped and done just that.

On the other side of the Mournes lies the idyllic Carlingford Lough area. Across the Lough in County Louth are the Cooley Mountains, the area that, according to Walter Hooper, Jack thought most resembled Narnia.[2] I have heard Jack's stepson, Douglas Gresham, say in public that the landscape of Narnia is the landscape of County Down. I do not doubt him, for County Down lay deep in Jack's consciousness all of his life. So it seems both County Down and County Louth contributed to the creation of Narnia.

Narnia really all began with a picture Jack had been carrying in his head. Since he was sixteen, he had visualised a faun carrying parcels and an umbrella in a snowy forest. In 1939, the little evacuee girl had asked what was inside the wardrobe at The Kilns. One day in 1948, Jack decided to write a story about the faun. The image was followed by another one of a queen on a sledge; and as he continued a lion came bounding into the story. He had recently been dreaming about lions. Jack did not set out to write Christian books for children, using his stories as a Christian allegory. He stated categorically that *The Chronicles of Narnia* is not an allegory. Basically he was trying to answer a question. He imagined a land like Narnia; and he wondered what would have happened if the Son of God, as He became a Man in our world, had come there as a Lion? Jack didn't know where the Lion came from, or even why he came; but it was the Lion who pulled the whole story of *The Lion, the Witch and the Wardrobe* together, and six more Narnian stories with it.

Jack did not believe that originality lies in the author of a book. He believed that a writer should not conceive of himself as bringing about beauty or wisdom that did not exist before. He believed a writer's art should embody a reflection of eternal beauty and wisdom. The writer was to be derivative, gaining his or her inspiration from another source and reflecting it as in a mirror. He believed the New Testament teaches that originality is God's prerogative alone, and that our writing is to be like clean mirrors, filled with the image of a face that is not our own. Changing metaphors, he saw himself as an adjective pointing to a noun.

So, in Aslan in *The Chronicles of Narnia*, we see the two great qualities which Jack found in the Lord Jesus: intolerable severity and irresistible tenderness. Mr. Beaver insisted that Aslan was not harmless and was not like a tame lion. His roar once shook all of Narnia, from the lamppost in the West to the shores of the Eastern Sea. When Aslan, the High King of Narnia, stooped towards Shasta, though, there was some "strange and solemn perfume"[3] that hung about his mane. That perfume has permeated *The Chronicles of Narnia*, and millions of children have smelled it. It is truly irresistible. Awe, power, and majesty grip the reader; it is pointing beyond this world of changing shadows to that which is fixed and eternal. The Shadowlands point to a light that is beyond that of the sun, moon, or stars.

Jack wrote five of *The Chronicles of Narnia* between the summers of 1948 and 1951. During this time, Shadowlands had been living up to its name. Janie Moore had had a stroke in 1944 that left her without the use of her left arm. As her age began to increase, she was often in pain from varicose veins and became quarrelsome, bad tempered, and difficult. Eventually she became senile. Warren's alcoholism did not help things, and on one particular binge in Ireland in June 1947 he was taken unconscious to Our Lady of Lourdes Hospital in Drogheda, County Louth. Jack received a telegram telling him of his brother's condition. He went straight to Ireland and stayed at the White Horse Inn for a week visiting his brother. The head of the Order at the hospital, Mother Mary Martin, who showed Warren great kindness, invited Jack to contribute an essay to a book that the hospital was soon to publish. He wrote an essay entitled "Some Thoughts." The man who had preached to the students at Oxford in 1939 that we always work on the edge of a precipice was still feeling the reality of what he preached. Drogheda was to become Warren's home-away-from-home for the rest of his life, and he attended the services at St. Peter's Church of Ireland in the town.

Warren continued to have severe drinking problems and was admitted to the Ackland Nursing Home in Oxford in February 1949, when Jack was halfway through writing *The Lion, the Witch and the Wardrobe*. By June 1949, Jack was in the Ackland himself, suffering, his doctor maintained, from exhaustion. Ordered to take a month's rest, Jack wrote to his friend Arthur Greeves to tell him that he was "coming home" to Belfast for a month; it is interesting to note that for Jack Lewis "home" was still Belfast. This was despite his public fame as a Christian apologist based in Oxford. *Time Magazine*, for example, had featured him on its front cover (8 September 1947) across the United States, and Professor Chad Walsh in the *Atlantic Monthly* (September 1946) had called him "the Apostle to the Sceptics." Despite his long association with Oxford and academia, when he was ordered to rest he wanted to go home. The landscape of Narnia was calling. Sadly, another drinking binge of Warren's prevented the journey.

Despite calls from at least two different American friends to take a holiday in the United States, Jack stayed closely tethered to his work. Warren settled down to continue his writing about seventeenth and eighteenth century France. He eventually had quite a few books published on the subject, and also read some of his work to The Inklings, who held him in deep affection. Jack was now well into his third Narnian story, *The Voyage of the Dawn Treader*.

The autumn of 1949 brought Jack one of his greatest disappointments. On Thursday evening, 27 October 1949, no one turned up for The Inklings' meeting. The Tuesday-morning gatherings continued, but one of the delights of Jack's life was over. Jack's comment that this life is but an inn by the side of the road proved to be true again and again. As he battled on for the cause of Christ's kingdom, the Thursday-evening gatherings of The Inklings had been a comfort and an inspiration to him. They had given him security, reassurance, and downright happiness.

"Many are the afflictions of the righteous, but the Lord delivers him out of them all," wrote the psalmist.[4] Another affliction Jack faced was the harsh response his friend J. R. R. Tolkien gave to *The Chronicles of Narnia*. He never liked them; it is reckoned that he considered them to be superficial and to have been written too hastily. When Jack read *The Lion, the Witch and the Wardrobe* to Tolkien in February 1949, he reacted by saying that Jack had made a mistake in assembling too many mythical creatures in Narnia. Tolkien didn't think it worked to have Father Christmas, a white witch, nymphs, fauns, and beavers all together in the same country. Since Jack held Tolkien's opinion in very high esteem, he reeled under his criticism.

The saviour of *The Chronicles of Narnia* turned out to be the Deputy Librarian of Merton College, Roger Lancelyn Green. The world owes Roger Green an incalculable debt. As a friend and former pupil of Jack's, he enthusiastically encouraged Jack's writing of *The Lion, the Witch and the Wardrobe*. Roger Green gave the book high praise without which Jack probably would never have even completed writing the book, let alone have it published. Other friends praised the book while Jack was writing it; but Roger Green is singled out for having the greatest influence. He is a shining example of the truth of "the power-of-one."

History is full of other examples of this truth. One vote gave Oliver Cromwell control of the United Kingdom. One vote caused Charles I to be executed. One vote brought Texas into the Union. One vote gave Adolf Hitler control of the Nazi party. One man's prayers (Moses') saved Israel from being abandoned by God. One pair of trained eyes gave the world penicillin. In 1928 Sir Alexander Fleming made the accidental discovery of a blue mould growing in a petri dish lying amongst a lot of other dishes on his bench. A crater on the moon was named after him—maybe they ought to name one after Roger Lancelyn Green for saving *The Chronicles of Narnia*.

But Lewis faced other afflictions at home. In April 1949, Janie Moore had fallen out of bed three times in one night, and consequently her situation needed constant attention. She was admitted to Restholme at 230 Woodstock Road,

Oxford, a nursing home run by a Miss Watson. Again, Jack's plans for a holiday in Ireland during 1950 were thwarted. He simply could not afford a holiday in addition to the cost of keeping Mrs. Moore in the nursing home. He visited the now senile Janie more or less daily. These were distressing visits, as Janie gradually returned to a state of infancy. She died on 12 June 1951 and was buried in the churchyard of Holy Trinity Church in Headington Quarry.

Janie Moore's death brought Jack Lewis release from a commitment that had lasted for thirty years. He was now free to visit friends, to travel more widely, and to escape the drudgeries of the past years of domestic life. He was also free to invite friends to stay with him at The Kilns. Yet there was something deeply mysterious about Jack's relationship with Janie Moore. In it is to be found the virtues of loyalty to a promise and incredible kindness. His love for her may have been *eros* to begin with, but it most certainly became and ended with *agape*.

As a sixteen-year-old, Jill Flewett arrived at The Kilns as an evacuee from London and spent two years there. She later wrote of the many happy times Janie and Jack had together, and how that Janie "adored him absolutely." Now Lady Jill Freud, wife of Sir Clement, she is on record as saying that Janie's "whole life was centred around him and around him alone. The running of the house, the cooking, the meals—everything she did was geared for Jack's happiness and comfort."[5] I take it that what Lady Freud wrote is absolutely true. The horrendous times of the First World War had brought Jack and Janie together; and there is something noble in the way Jack protected and cared for Janie for the rest of her earthly life. If ever loyalty was tested, it was in Jack Lewis, and he came through with flying colours.

Loss of The Inklings' Thursday-evening meeting, loss of Janie Moore, criticism of his writing by one whom he honoured, Warren's drinking binges—could there be any more disappointment for him? It came in the form of academic disappointment. Jack had already been championed by Tolkien for the Merton Professorship of Modern English Literature, but he discovered that other electors were against Jack. They pointed out that his most successful books were three novels and some popular religious or theological books. They thought his election would lower the status of the professorship, and even discredit the English school. When the Professorship of Poetry fell vacant, several of Jack's friends nominated him. Again there was opposition, amongst other reasons for his up-front preaching of Christianity. One particular academic, who strongly disliked Jack's Ulster background, skilfully used University politics and moved against him. Out of the thousands who were eligible to do so, less than four hundred of the Senior Members of the University voted, and the Professorship went to C. Day Lewis, who won by nineteen votes. Warren recorded in his diary that he was astonished at the virulence of the anti-Christian feeling.

There were many admirable qualities in Jack's Christian life, but one of the most commendable was his lack of bitterness in the face of disappointment. He could have lashed out against his critics, or turned in upon himself and become sour in spirit and full of self-pity. There was none of this. In a time of loss and disappointment, he proved the truth of Isaiah's great statement about God:

> He gives power to the weak, and to those who have no might he increases strength. Even the youths shall faint and be weary, and the young men shall utterly fall; but those who

> wait on the Lord shall renew their strength; they shall mount up with wings as eagles, they shall run and not be weary, they shall walk and not faint.[6]

Even as Jack waited for trains, he had a practise of walking up and down the platform praying to the Lord. Such people soar, even in turbulent winds. In fact, turbulent winds seem to enable them to soar even higher. It is important to remember that some of the exquisite passages in *The Chronicles of Narnia* were written at a time of bleak crosswinds in the life of their author. This fact proves again the biblical truth that, although all things that happen to those who love God are not good in and of themselves, they always *work together for good*.[7]

In March 1951, Jack returned home to Northern Ireland. He stayed in the little County Down village of Crawfordsburn, near Bangor, where his friend Arthur Greeves had a cottage. Jack enjoyed staying at the seventeenth century "Old Inn," which still enjoys a favourable reputation in the twenty-first century. Throughout the centuries it has played host to highwaymen, presidents, pop stars, and even Tsar Peter the Great. This time, it sheltered the creator of Narnia. Around him were the Holywood hills, and his spirit was deeply refreshed as he walked once more in his childhood haunts. He was home.

Beginning in the Michaelmas Term of 1951, Magdalen College gave Jack a sabbatical year. Its purpose was to let him complete volume three of *The Oxford History of English Literature*, entitled *English Literature in the Sixteenth Century, Excluding Drama*. The work involved a mountain of reading in the Duke Humfrey's Library, part of the Bodleian in Oxford. Jack read the complete works of about two hundred authors, including the entire works of Luther, Calvin, Sir Thomas More, and Tyndale.

The book was a *tour de force*. It was radical, controversial, startling, deeply thoughtful, witty, and humorous. It was also compellingly readable in its magnificent sweep across sixteenth century English literature. From the point of view of Christianity, its third chapter holds great interest, since in it Jack looks in detail at "religious controversy and translation," and how the sixteenth-century text reads on the page. He presents his opinion of the writing of leaders like Tyndale, Latimer, Cranmer, John Knox, Sir Thomas More, Richard Hooker, John Foxe, Cardinal William Allen, and John Donne. Jack shows that the Puritans, who wished to abolish episcopacy and remodel the Church of England on the terms which Calvin had laid down in Geneva, had doctrines not of terror but of joy and hope; and that the experience of the Reformation was one of relief and buoyancy. In the entire work, some literature was debunked and some exalted. John Donne was put in the caste of a minor poet. Shakespeare's *Venus and Adonis* is not highly praised; his sonnets, though, receive very high accolades.

The book got some excellent reviews; but for me the most adroit and perceptive summary was given in the *Oxford Magazine*:

> I have often heard Lewis's excursions into what has been called popular theology adversely commented upon, and sometimes even with the suggestion that he was neglecting his proper business. I will express no opinion upon these activities, but I will insist that this book is not only a triumphant refutation of the view that they have been a mere distraction, but a triumphant justification of the interests and studies that have lain behind them.[8]

Sir Winston Churchill obviously did not think Jack had been neglecting his proper business. In the King's Honours List of 1951 he offered Jack a CBE.[9] It was Warren who wrote of the reason for Jack's refusal of this high honour. He said, "Jack felt obliged to refuse this: his appearance in a Conservative Honours List might, he felt, strengthen the ill-founded case of those who identified religious writing with anti-leftist propaganda."[10]

By August 1951, when Jack was holidaying again at the Crawfordsburn Inn, *The Lion, the Witch and the Wardrobe* had been published, and he had finished writing *Prince Caspian, The Voyage of the Dawn Treader, The Silver Chair,* and *The Horse and His Boy. The Magician's Nephew* had already been started. He, who had spoken of the coming arctic wind of old age, was finding instead that God had given him a breath of spring. When certain central features of his life had come to an end, this was a time of new beginnings. God never ends with an end, of course; He always ends with a beginning. The following year was to bring Jack the sort of beginning that any confirmed bachelor would have laughed off.

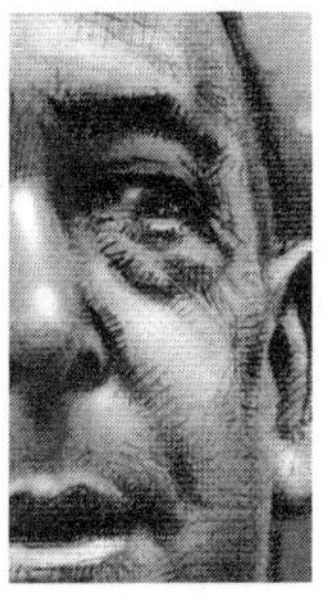

Chapter Sixteen

NO LONGER FACELESS

September 1952 was revealing a post-harvest England. As the pearly-grey morning mists lifted, they revealed the tiny flowers on the margins of the stubbled fields. These little flowers—the mayweed, pimpernel, charlock, bindweed, and the field forget-me-not—were flourishing now that the harvest had been cleared. In the meadows, some plants were still prominent: hardheads, agrimony, false fox sedge, and bristly ox-tongue.

In the now fast-receding summer, children could be found wandering along the hedges with half-filled baskets and purple-stained mouths. Few of them could resist the temptation to eat the blackberries rather than gather them. Thousands upon thousands of bushes carried the succulent fruit.

As the September days shortened, all kinds of birds were busy. The sweet little song of the swallow was soothing and healing to minds and hearts. Flocks of skylarks, hedge sparrows, starlings, and linnets circled the fields and hedgerows, dropping in a body as soon as anything worth eating was spotted. It did not take much to alarm them; suddenly, on being disturbed, they would rise up as a cloud only to sink down again at a safer end of the stubble-filled field.

On 24 September 1952, an Anglophile from New York arrived at Jack's Magdalen College rooms. She was to bring Jack an incredible amount of love and happiness. He admitted that what he thought he would have had in his twenties he had in his sixties. Even to his own surprise, he was going to fall in love.

I have long wondered what she was really like. I have stayed at her son's house and talked to him about his relationship with Jack. I have also discussed with him the love story that developed between his mother and Jack. In his home I have looked at her photograph looking at me, and have pondered on her personality. Deborah Winger, of course, gave the famous interpretation of her personality in the film *Shadowlands*. Claire Bloom has attempted the interpretation on stage; but to understand her personality more deeply, one needs to understand her roots and history.

Joy Gresham was born Joy Davidman in New York City on 18 April 1915. Her Jewish parents came from Eastern Europe. Her father, Joseph Isaac Davidman, was born in Poland in 1887 and immigrated to New York in 1893. Her mother, Jeanette Davidman, came from the Ukraine. Joy's parents had abandoned their Jewish faith; but, because of conversations she had with her mother as she grew up, its legacy remained long in Joy's mind. Her mother would tell her in detail of Jewish-Ukrainian village life; one imagines it to be similar to the film *Fiddler on the Roof*.

Joy took a B.A. at Hunter College, New York in 1934, and an M.A. in English Literature at Columbia University in 1935, when she was just twenty. For a few years she taught

English in various high schools in New York. She has left the following record of her early thinking:

> In 1929 I believed in nothing but American prosperity; in 1930 I believed in nothing. Men, I said, are only apes. Virtue is only custom. Life is only an electrochemical reaction. Mind is only a set of conditioned reflexes, and anyway most people aren't rational like me. Love, art, and altruism are only sex. The universe is only matter. Matter is only energy. I forget what I said energy was only.[1]

The atheistic Joy lived in New York at a grim time in the life of the nation. Following the Wall Street Crash, depression was gripping the United States. In an unprecedented wave of panic, fear, and confusion, thirteen million shares changed hands on the New York Stock Exchange in one day, 24 October 1929. As Joy saw hungry men selling apples on the street corners of New York, she felt she could not be indifferent to the needs of others. She decided to join the Communist Party. The Party sent her to work on their magazine *New Masses*. Her talent as a poet was recognised when her book of free verse, *Letter to a Comrade,* was published. It won the Yale Younger Poets award for 1938. Encouraged, Joy left school-teaching and spent six months as a junior scriptwriter for MGM in Hollywood.

In 1940, Joy Davidman's novel *Anya* was published, and it showed the evidence of those avid conversations with her mother before the Second World War.

In Britain, we have the wonderful *Rabbi Mark* stories by David Kossoff, which describe Jewish life in Poland before the First World War. They are jewels of wisdom, sparkling with Jewish humour. I have never heard anyone equal David Kossoff's gift for public story telling.

Joy's novel about Ukrainian-Jewish village life tells the story of a shopkeeper's daughter who, in her search for free love, rebels against the narrow strictures of her Jewish upbringing. Since Joy was a woman who never had to follow those strictures in her youth, the novel says a lot about the depth of those mother-daughter conversations.

While editing a volume of anti-imperialist war poetry, *War Poems of the United Nations,* Joy met William Lindsay (Bill) Gresham. Six years older than Joy, Bill Gresham was already divorced and had gone to "fight" in the Spanish Civil War. He had returned mentally ill, survived an attempt at suicide, and had joined the Communist Party. Psychoanalysis treatment had helped his illness, and when Joy met him he was editor of a fiction magazine. The two were married in August 1942. Bill then worked as a freelance writer. He was an alcoholic. Their two boys, David and Douglas, were born in 1944 and 1945. They moved to Ossining, New York in 1946, by which time Bill was having an extra-marital affair, and his mental illness had returned with a vengeance. Both Joy and Bill had gotten help through Jack's publications; and both had professed faith in Christ in 1948. They also joined a local Presbyterian Church in Ossining. Joy eventually persuaded Bill to buy a farm in Staatsburg, New York, and he did with the proceeds based on the film of his thriller novel, *Nightmare Alley,* starring Tyrone Power.

In the latter part of 1949, Joy came across her friend Chad Walsh's book *C. S. Lewis: Apostle to the Sceptics*. Chad Walsh was a gifted poet and teacher, and eventually became Professor of English at Beloit College, Wisconsin. He met C. S. Lewis during the summer of 1948, and his book was the first to be written about Jack. It is still highly acclaimed. He was also ordained in the Episcopal Church, and served as an assistant at St. Paul's Church, Beliot, from 1948 to 1977. Joy talked with Chad about Jack and how she would like to know the answer to some of the points he raised. She could not have talked to a better man in America on the subject of Jack; Chad suggested that she write to him. In 1949, Joy also attended one or two lectures in New York by a friend of hers, a Roman Catholic priest named Victor White. The lectures were on the relationship between psychology and religion. Joy got into a discussion about C. S. Lewis with the lecturer, and he also advised her to write to Lewis.

So began one of the most intriguing and complex relationships of the twentieth-century literary world. Joy's was no average mind, and as we have already discovered in this story, neither was Jack's. The sparks of Jewish humour and abrasive New York manner soon lit up Joy's gifted writing in Jack's mind. Her marriage to Bill Gresham was falling apart. Both Joy and Bill were disillusioned by communism. Bill converted to Dianetics, a system developed by the founder of the Church of Scientology, L. Ron Hubbard, and then he got into Zen Buddhism and began to use tarot cards. His womanising continued, as did his irresponsibility with money.

Joy decided that she wanted to visit Jack in Oxford to ask his advice on her marriage and to discuss a book she was writing entitled *Smoke on the Mountain: An Interpretation of the Ten Commandments*. Did she, as we say in Ulster, "set her hat" for him? Such a question is perhaps too deep for any biographer to answer. She certainly looked up to him intellectually, and her admiration was no doubt mixed with a certain amount of awe. She certainly set great store by his point of view, and in her distress she knew he would give her honest counsel. He had, after all, been used by God to lead her to faith in Christ.

Seeking a safe place from her own alcoholic husband, Joy's cousin Renee Pierce and her two young children had come from Florida to live at the large Gresham home in Staatsburg, New York. The place must have been a veritable pressure cooker. At that time, Joy received an invitation to visit a pen pal called Phyllis Williams in London. Renee said she would look after Joy's family while she was gone, so Joy decided to go to England. She crossed the Atlantic from New York, docked at Liverpool, and eventually arrived to stay with Phyllis in August 1952. From there she wrote to Jack, inviting him to lunch with her and with Phyllis on 24 September, at the East Gate Hotel, across the street from Magdalen College. Jack wrote back to invite them both to lunch at his Magdalen College rooms.

Jack's friend, George Sayer, has written about the meeting. Since Warren had withdrawn, George was invited to take his place. Joy was no shrinking violet, and she exploded into Jack's life. George Sayer thought the meeting was a real success. Joy was physically attractive, sharp-featured, dark-haired, blunt, distinctly anti-urban, and clearly anti-American. This abrasive New Yorker with a passion for small-farm life was going to influence Jack Lewis far more deeply than he realised. When Jack led the party around his college, Joy, uninhibited by her surroundings, fired off impudent questions that brought howls of laughter in response.

Further meetings with Joy followed; and on 6 December 1952, Jack invited her to stay at The Kilns for Christmas. While she was there, a letter arrived from her husband suggesting a divorce. He said that he and her cousin were in love; he now wanted to marry Renee. After a divorce, Joy would be free to marry someone else, and they could all live within calling distance of each other.

Joy discussed the letter with Jack, and he advised her to divorce Bill. So Joy returned to the United States; but she returned to even worse horrors, because Bill was drinking again and was Renee's sexual partner. Now very low in finances, Joy stayed on to pay off family debts. At the beginning of 1953, she was confirmed in the Episcopal Church in the Cathedral of St. John the Divine in New York. She then started saving to raise funds for a return to England.

As for Jack, what one can only call "the fountain of life springing up within him" was as fresh as ever. The fifth story in the *Chronicles of Narnia* series, *The Horse and His Boy*, was at the publishers by March 1953; and Jack was busy proof-reading *English Language in the Sixteenth Century*. He finished writing the last of the *Chronicles of Narnia, The Last Battle*.

In November 1953, Joy Gresham returned to England with her two boys, and they stayed for four days in December with Jack and Warren at The Kilns. Joy settled her boys at Dane Court Preparatory School in Surrey. For the next eighteen months, things were fairly quiet between Jack and Joy; but they certainly were not quiet between Jack and academia. The talk of the Common Rooms was that Jack had accepted the offer of the newly appointed Chair of Medieval and Renaissance English at Cambridge University. As with most things in Jack's life, the path to this appointment had not been smooth. He'd been pleased, honoured, and overjoyed at the invitation; but he was concerned for the welfare of his gardener Paxford and his brother Warren, if Jack moved to Cambridge. He was reluctant to accept, until J. R. R. Tolkien, who thought Jack had not been treated well by Oxford, powerfully intervened. Tolkien was determined that Jack should have the Chair at Cambridge. Lewis had now been passed over for three Chairs at Oxford. Professor Helen Gardner, in her obituary of C. S. Lewis for the British Academy, makes no bones about the fact that what Jack himself called his "hot-gospeling" had encouraged these "pass-overs."

On 17 May, Tolkien, who was one of the electors for the Chair, had a long conversation with Jack and convinced him that he would not be letting Paxford and Warren down by going to Cambridge. He convinced Jack that he could keep his home in Oxford and still work at Cambridge. Jack's friends at Cambridge suggested that he could reside at Cambridge from Monday to Friday, and spend the weekends, Monday mornings, and the whole of his holidays elsewhere. Further correspondence between Jack and Sir Henry Willink, the Vice-Chancellor of Cambridge University, brought the whole matter to a satisfactory conclusion. On 4 June 1954, he wrote to Sir Henry expressing pleasure and gratitude in accepting the Chair of Medieval and Renaissance English.

The summer of 1954 saw Jack and Warren back in the South of Ireland on holiday; afterwards Jack went to spend time with his friend Arthur Greeves at Crawfordsburn. On 16 September, Lewis's incisive work *English Language in the sixteenth Century* was published.

On 29 November 1954—his fifty-sixth birthday—Jack gave his inaugural lecture *De Description Temporum* at Cambridge in the largest lecture hall in Mill Lane. When a party of his friends and former pupils arrived, they couldn't find seats in the lecture hall and had to sit on the dais behind him. They were claiming kinship in the hour of power, so to speak! Gowned and capped university dons lined the front rows, and a new generation of undergraduates leaned forward to savour the mind of this Ulsterman, who was famous not only for his academic prowess but also concerning the name of the Lord.

If any had thought they were going to hear a lecture being played to a gallery who wanted more in-depth-study of modern literature in universities, they would have been disappointed. Passionately, amusingly, brilliantly, Jack attacked the "new" myth that new is better. He made a defence for the study of Old Western Literature, and firmly identified himself as an Old Western Man. He even referred to himself as one of the few remaining dinosaurs—a useful specimen of an old order. He unashamedly spoke of post-Christian Europe. He caused quite an intellectual stir, and received thunderous applause. It must have been a great day for him, given his great disappointment that younger dons at Oxford were pushing for the study of more modern literature, to the reduction of the study of Old English. Now, he was the new Professor of Medieval and Renaissance English at Cambridge. The Old Western Man had a new castle in which he was the liege lord!

Situated by the River Cam, Magdalene College was founded in 1428 as a Benedictine hostel before being re-founded in 1542 as the College of St. Mary Magdalene, a constituent college of the University of Cambridge. The re-foundation of the college was largely the work of Sir Thomas Audley, the Lord Chancellor under Henry VIII. Sir Thomas gave Magdalene its motto: *Garde ta Foy*, meaning "Keep your Faith." The Faculty of Divinity at Cambridge University had been at the cutting edge of research in theology and religious studies for eight hundred years; but the new Professor of English, who took up residence at Magdalene College on 1 January 1955, was keeping his faith in a different arena.

Through his writing, Jack's voice was now being heard very clearly. On 19 September his autobiography, *Surprised by Joy,* was published. It was the story of his conversion. The

Chronicles of Narnia, and the task of writing *English Language in the Sixteenth Century,* had interrupted its writing. Although it is as intriguing for what it leaves out as for what it leaves in, there can be few autobiographies to equal it for candour. We can be certain that Jack had found his voice. How the book preaches! Preaches? Of course it preaches. On Saturday, 5 November 1955, Jack was invited along with other Senior Members of the University to meet Dr. Billy Graham, who was in Cambridge to lead a mission for the Cambridge Inter-Collegiate Christian Union. It was the same Dr. Graham who said, "You are not really preaching until they hear another voice." Few people reading *Surprised by Joy* lay it down without hearing that other voice. So, by that standard, the book truly preaches.

In July 1955, Jack Lewis was elected as a member of the British Academy; and as the new term started at Cambridge he got his driver-friend, Clifford Morris, to take him there. Clifford relates that, on his way to Cambridge, Jack loved to be taken to see the herds of deer in Woburn Park, the Duke of Bedford's great estate in Berkshire.[2]

At the beginning of the new term in 1955 with Professor Lewis, let us pause and muse a little. In July 2002, I stood on a hill in Woburn Park above Woburn Abbey and mused a little myself. With two friends I had just been filming a video on the life of John Bunyan. The Tinker of Bedford and his amazing story of Christian's pilgrimage in *Pilgrim's Progress* had inspired my heart and soul. (Incidentally, on 11 September 1962, the BBC recorded Jack reading an essay on Bunyan's *Pilgrim's Progress.*) When I got home, the emotions of standing on that hill above Woburn Abbey were recollected in tranquillity. I share them with you:

"Sunset At Woburn"

I stood on a height at Woburn,
Evening sunlight dipped as swallows arched home
To the eaves of the ancient and distinguished Abbey,
Where the flag of the Dukes of Bedford fluttered.
Away across the long-shadowed forest glades,
Stags called and hinds stirred,
And baby deer darted as the sun set.
And I thought of the Tinker of Bedford,
That humble mender of pots and pans,
And his visits to the house of John Gifford,
And of how his soul panted for spiritual life,
Like a hart after the water brook.
And I marvelled at Gifford's patience
Over those many question-filled hours,
As John Bunyan sought salvation in Christ
And found it, so memorably.
And I thought of his book The Pilgrims Progress,
And the millions who have drunk
At its deep spiritual waters.
I mused on how a former Duke of Bedford
Generously raised Bunyan's statue in Bedford.
Ah! Not many mighty, not many of noble birth
Are called: but God has chosen the weak things,
And the things which are despised of this world,
To put to shame the things that are mighty,
So that no one may boast before Him.

Despite what I have just written, I feel it is so necessary to add one thing to my musings. The Bible text does say, "not *many* mighty are called"; how glad I am that it does not say "not *any* mighty."

One of the "mighty," now beginning a new term of his great work at Cambridge University, had clearly been called. He had only seven years of his earthly pilgrimage left. Unbeknownst to him, before they were through he was to know great joy, and deep, indescribable sorrow.

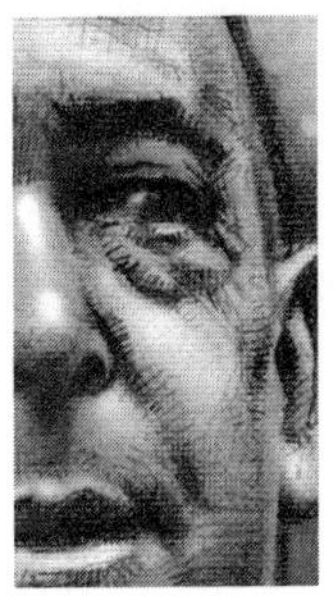

Chapter Seventeen

THE BRIDEGROOM AND THE WIDOWER

Spring was spreading across England with all of its enchanting loveliness. There was fresh colour everywhere. Winter's bare outline had been softened to the green mist of breaking buds and billions of unfolding leaves; blue, green, and gold were fusing into a general brightness. In copse and lane, primroses were wafting their sweet, fresh, wholesome scent. Regal swans were returning to their favourite pools and rivers. Water rats could be heard plopping enthusiastically into the water, and screeching moorhens and ducks were busy among the reed-beds.

In England, April is the month for much bird-nesting activity. House martins, wrens, willow-warblers, chaffinches, and yellow hammers were hard at work. Perhaps the making of the chaffinch's nest is the most delicate operation of them all. The sturdy, cheerful little chaffinch gathers moss, down, wood, hair, and wool, and binds them all together with consummate skill.

House martins were looking longingly for April rain, for they needed mud for the masonry of their nests. They didn't want too much, though! Then they needed sun and wind to harden and set the mud. Swallows were equally busy, carrying thousands of mud pellets to make the mud-cup cradles so familiar beneath the eaves of English homes. On Monday 23 April 1956, the activities down at the little Register Office in St. Giles, Oxford could hardly have been called "nest-building". What was going on?

Back in August 1955, Joy Gresham and her boys had set up home on High Street in Headington, about a mile from The Kilns. Jack leased the house, and he also paid the rent. In September 1955, Jack was back in Ireland on holiday and raised the matter of his relationship with Joy with his friend Arthur Greeves. The Home Office had refused Joy permission to live and work in England, and Jack now proposed the idea of going through a civil marriage ceremony in order to give British nationality to Joy, David, and Douglas. Jack regarded it as a merely legal formality, and not as a marriage before God. He intended to tell as few people as possible. There is no record of what Arthur Greeves thought; but his Roman Catholic friend George Sayer raised serious objections. Jack maintained that he was not in love with Joy and did not see the arrangement as a real marriage. He viewed it as a way to help out a friend.

Jack's doctor, R. E. Harvard, and Austin Farrer, the philosopher, theologian, and Chaplain of Trinity College, were present at the ceremony as witnesses. The scene was famously portrayed in the film *Shadowlands*, with Jack going one way and Joy another as they came out of the Register Office into a rain-swept day in Oxford. The scene may not have been factually correct; but one feels it may have been accurate in its portrayal of Jack's emotions.

Jack now started to visit Joy every day, and Joy protested that the visits would cause a scandal. She put him under pressure to allow her and the boys to live at The Kilns. She was certainly in love with Jack; but he was not in love with her—yet. How would such a complex relationship ever resolve itself?

There is an Irish saying, "It's a long road that has no turning." The turning on the road that Jack and Joy were travelling came unexpectedly, with a telephone call. For some time Joy had been complaining of pains in her chest, back, and left leg. On the evening of the eighteenth of October 1956, Kathleen Farrer, novelist and wife of the Chaplain of Trinity College, had a premonition. Feeling sure that something was wrong with Joy, she telephoned her. As it happened, just before the telephone rang out, Joy had tripped over the telephone wire and fallen to the floor, bringing the telephone down as she fell. The femur of her left leg had snapped in two. As the phone lay on the floor, Joy could hear Kathleen's voice asking with concern if there was anything she could do. The next day, Joy was admitted to the Wingfield-Morris Orthopaedic Hospital. Examination and x-rays proved that Joy had cancer, and that it had eaten almost completely through her femur. This was not the only bad news. Examination also discovered that she had a malignant tumour in her left breast and secondary sites in her right leg and shoulder. Within the next month, Joy had three operations: the tumour was removed, the cancerous part of the femur was cut out and the bone repaired, and her ovaries were removed.

Jack now had to face the fact that Joy was almost certainly dying; and he wanted to bring her home to The Kilns, where she could die as his wife. He set about seeking a Christian marriage ceremony and had great difficulty. The Bishop of Oxford, although sympathetic, refused to give permission for one of his clergymen to marry them. The rule in the Church of England was that it would not remarry divorced persons. Even Jack's friends on the University faculty said no. Eventually, another Anglican clergyman, a former pupil of Jack's, agreed to help them. Jack took the view that, since Bill Gresham had been divorced before he married Joy, and since his former wife was still alive, Bill's marriage to Joy was not a Christian marriage.

The Reverend Peter Bide from the diocese of Chesterfield performed the ceremony. The night before Peter laid his hands on Joy for her healing. He is on record as saying that for him, what clinched the argument as to whether he should conduct the wedding ceremony was considering what the Lord would have done in the situation.

Alone in his room at The Kilns that night, what were Jack's thoughts as he went to bed? In my opinion he must have felt very vulnerable because of his great compassion and considerable international fame. What he had just done was full of perplexing questions. Could he really have put his head on his pillow in a carefree manner? Some of the Greek tragedies that he knew so well were not all that far removed from his own situation. In the secret chamber of his heart, how did he feel?

It does not seem to me that Jack was as yet in love with Joy. I am reminded of what my mother used to tell me: Pity is akin to love. The situation that developed between Jack and Joy proves her to be right, I think. If Jack's relationship with Janie Moore began with *eros* and ended with *agape*, his relationship with Joy began with *agape* and certainly ended with *eros*. He actually told a friend that, though it began with *agape*, it proceeded to *philia*, then became pity, and then finally became *eros*.[1]

As Death threatened to take his wife, Jack suddenly woke up to what he would lose. His rival, Death, awakened love in his heart.[2] There is no question that now he began to fall deeply in love with Joy.

In 1956, Joy was sent home to The Kilns to die. It was thought that she had only weeks to live; but little by little, she began to improve. She was able to walk in the house, then in the garden, and before long Jack was able to leave her in Warren's care while he was in Cambridge. I find Joy to be an enigmatic woman, one of great intellectual ability. Perhaps the most moving and interesting tribute to her comes from Warren Lewis. In his affectionate and honouring *Memoir of C. S. Lewis* given in his introduction to Jack's published letters, he comments that it was a delight to watch Jack and Joy together. He wrote, "For me Jack's marriage meant that our home was enriched and enlivened by the presence of a witty, broad-minded, well-read, and tolerant Christian, whom I had rarely heard equalled as a conversationalist, and whose company was a never-ending source of enjoyment."[3]

At this time in Joy's life, Jack suffered from osteoporosis. While he was losing calcium from his bones, Joy was gaining it in hers. He had prayed that God would allow him to take her pain, and he believed that this had happened. He was fitted with a surgical brace that supported his weakened spine, and he wore it for the rest of his life.

Amazingly, all through this stressful time Jack's pen flowed. He wrote a book called *Reflections on the Psalms*. By the New Year, Joy was redecorating The Kilns, cleaning and repainting. She was able to go out driving and was rushing about her home with a new zest for living. That zest encouraged them to have a belated honeymoon in County Down and County Donegal.

It was Jack's first flight in an aircraft when in July they flew to Belfast, the Professor terrified at the take-off, enchanted by his first above-the-clouds experience, and excited at the first glimpse of the Irish coastline. At the airport, they were met by the ever-faithful Arthur Greeves and driven to The Old Inn at Crawfordsburn, where they stayed for a fortnight. The Inn sits right on the edge of a wooded country park that sweeps down to the shores of Belfast Lough. Throughout the week they explored County Down and County Louth in Arthur's car; and Jack gave a dinner at The Old Inn to introduce Joy to his relations. One wonders what Flora and Albert would have made of it all. Jack's relatives took very well to Joy. After Crawfordsburn, they went to the Royal Fort Hotel in Rathmullan, County Donegal, and returned to Oxford, as Jack put it "drunk with blue mountains, yellow beaches, dark fuchsia, breaking waves, braying donkeys, peat-smell, and the heather just beginning to bloom."[4] The landscape of Narnia was still able to cast its spell.

In 1957, Jack had been asked to make some recordings for the Episcopal Radio-TV Foundation of Atlanta, Georgia. He chose as his subject the four loves, which he called Affection, Friendship, Eros, and Charity. His scripts were finished by the end of the summer of 1958, and Jack went to London to meet the founder of the American organisation, Mrs. Caroline Rakestraw, and to record his talks. They did not get on well. Mrs. Rakestraw tried to change his scripts and singularly failed. The organisation then began a significant advertising campaign, giving the impression that Jack would be in America to deliver the talks. However, when the Episcopalian Bishops on the board of the Foundation met, they decided that Jack's talks were too frank for American audiences. Mrs. Rakestraw flew back to London to explain. The problem was, she said, that Jack had brought sex into his talk on *eros*. Jack wanted to know how he could talk about *eros* and leave it out!

In the end, the recordings were offered to radio stations outside Mrs. Rakestraw's network, though they were not widely broadcast. The actual recordings themselves fell far below the standard of Jack's former BBC recordings. The honing skills of James Welch and his assistant, Eric Fern, were patently missing.

In the Bible story of Samson, we learn that Samson ate honey out of the carcass of a dead lion. So often in Jack's life, good things came out of unusual situations. The seemingly dead broadcasts eventually emerged as one of his best books. Jack had been given freedom to use the radio script as the basis for a book, *The Four Loves*. In the blurb of the book the *Church Times* commented, "He has never written better. Nearly every page scintillates with observations which are illuminating, provocative, and original."[5]

The book looks at affection, friendship, *eros*, and charity. Lewis shows that the first three need the sweetening grace of charity, God's love, which loves the unlovable. As for his dealing with sex, who could not be thankful for Lewis's honesty that exposes a lustful man's care for the pleasure of sex rather than the woman who gives it. Only a writer like Jack Lewis would illustrate such beastly behaviour by pointing out that the smoker does not keep the carton after he has smoked his cigarette. How much better is *eros* if it does not desire the Beloved herself but merely the pleasure she can give?

Jack shows that, unredeemed, *eros* can be poisonous. I've never read a more powerful novel than Count Leo Tolstoy's *Anna Karenina*. Considered by many to be the world's greatest novel, it employs Tolstoy's intense imaginative insight to create some of the most memorable characters in literature. Jack uses this story to show how dangerous *eros* can be if not controlled. It certainly led Anna to abandon her child Seryozha and her husband Alexei for Count Vronsky. Tolstoy's description of the fallen Anna, stealing back into her former home to see her son on his birthday, is a narrative of heartbreaking intensity. Her eventual suicide, chillingly and hauntingly described by Tolstoy like no other piece of literature I have ever encountered, shows where uncontrolled *eros* can lead.

Jack shows that Affection, Friendship, and Eros all die or become demons, unless they obey God. No doubt, *The Four Loves* was deeply affected by his ever-deepening love for Joy. We must be thankful that the disappointment over the broadcasts on *The Four Loves* did not lead him to abandon his book.

In September 1958, Jack's book *Reflections on the Psalms* was published. It had been written in the autumn of 1957. Through his attendance at college chapel every morning, Jack came to know the Psalms almost by heart. He used the translation of the Psalms that is to be found in the Book of Common Prayer, the translation which was the work of Coverdale (1488-1568). Jack greatly admired the beauty and poetry of Coverdale's translation. In his book on the Psalms, he addresses themes such as the cursings, judgment in the Psalms, death, connivance, nature, and the fair beauty of the Lord.[6] He looks at how we ought to behave towards people in high positions who lie and behave abominably. With simplicity of style and at times undisguised wit, he confronts many of the knotty problems faced by any reader of the Psalms.

Following the publication of his book on the Psalms, Jack received an invitation from the Archbishop of Canterbury to become a member of the Commission to Revise the Psalter. He accepted and joined the committee of seven men—one of whom was T. S. Eliot. They revised the translation of the Psalms in the Church of England's

Book of Common Prayer. The completed version of this committee's work appeared in 1963 as *The Revised Psalter*.

Christmas 1958 came with a virtual snowstorm of thousands of Christmas cards falling on The Kilns. Across the world the name of C. S. Lewis was being established in the minds and hearts of many readers whom Jack could never know personally. They sent him cards with a loving vengeance!

Jack's married life was now at its apex. Joy, David, Douglas, and Jack turned to a new year with a very contented home hearth. It was by no means quiet, though. The banter between Jack and Joy was good-humoured, but Joy's occasional shooting of pigeons in the woods at The Kilns was not really to Jack's liking. She ate them, too!

Jack turned again to his work at Cambridge, lecturing twice a week giving a lecture titled "The Prolegomena to the Study of Our Earlier Poetry." In June, Joy and he returned to Northern Ireland and The Old Inn at Crawfordsburn once more, and to a week in Rathmullan, County Donegal with Arthur Greeves. They went to Wales for a summer break with David and Douglas, and then Jack returned to Cambridge to begin his lectures, "English Literature 1300-1500."

On 13 October, Jack returned to Oxford to take his wife for a routine check-up at the Churchill Hospital. The results revealed that cancerous spots had returned in many of her bones. It was deeply depressing news. Just when their marriage had reached a real depth of personal happiness for them both, suffering returned to fill their days with its pain and uncertainty.

Joy now entered a course of radiotherapy; and Jack continued his busy schedule of lectures at Cambridge University, especially enjoying eight lectures on Edmund Spenser's *Faerie Queene*. He saw Joy at weekends. How bittersweet his life must have been. He was still working on the edge of a precipice.

Joy showed great courage and cheerfulness during her final illness. In April 1960, she and Jack travelled to Greece with their friends Roger and June Lancelyn Green. Joy was dying, but she was able to realise her greatest lifelong desire. She climbed up to the Acropolis in Athens, and sat with Jack on the steps of the Propylaea, enjoying the beauty of the Parthenon and Erechtheum. Under an azure sky, they feasted their eyes on the honey-gold columns of Ancient Greece. They went to Mycenae and the Lion Gate. The party drove down through vineyards, scented pinewoods, and olive groves to the head of the Gulf of Corinth, and explored the ruins at Aegosthena. They dined on octopus, fried red mullet, fried squid, ewes' milk, cheese, fresh oranges, and they drank retsina in a little taverna right on the shores of the Gulf. They ate and talked by the lapping waves for several hours, surrounded by the hum of bees. Jack looked upon it as one of the greatest days of his life.[7]

They flew to Rhodes and visited Lindos, and attended an Easter Service at the Orthodox Church. They flew to Crete and visited the Palace of Nimos at Knossos. Then they flew to Pisa in Italy, staying for a night before returning to London on 13 April. For a classical scholar like Jack Lewis, the trip to the places he had been reading about for fifty years must have been deeply inspirational. They both must have known that Joy's life was ebbing, and therefore they relished the trip all the more.

The bliss of Greece was soon exchanged for the misery of cancer. In May, it reappeared in Joy's right breast, and after surgery she came back home to The Kilns. She could now get around only in a wheelchair; and, on Tuesday the fourteenth of June, Warren took her for what he thought was going to be her last outing. They went as far as the pond at The Kilns. On 20

June, she was taken to the Ackland Nursing Home, seemingly close to death, and Douglas was brought home from his school in Wales. But she recovered enough to return to The Kilns. On 3 July, she accompanied Jack to dinner at what was one of his favourite hotels, the Studley Priory; and the next day she went for a drive in the Cotswolds with her nurse.

On 12 July, Jack and Joy were playing scrabble together before bed; but at six o'clock the next morning the household was wakened by Joy's screaming. Jack called the doctor, and Joy was taken by ambulance to the Radcliffe Infirmary. Conscious to the last, Joy told the Chaplain that she was at peace with God. She died peacefully about 11.20 that evening.

For Jack, Warren, Douglas, and David it must have been a sombre taxi ride on Monday 18 July to the crematorium. The Chaplain of Trinity College Oxford, Austin Farrer, conducted a Christian service there. Joy's ashes were scattered at the Oxford Crematorium, and a marble plaque was erected, with Jack's special epitaph for her:

Here the whole world (stars, water, air,
And field, and forest, as they were
Reflected in a single mind)
Like cast-off clothes was left behind
In ashes yet with hope that she,
In lenten lands, hereafter may
Resume them on her Easter Day.

There is a story told of Napoleon Bonaparte who, when approached by one of his officers to promote a soldier who had distinguished himself in battle, answered, "And what did he do the next day?"

Napoleon would have been intrigued by what Jack Lewis did on the day following the death of his wife. Donald Swann (of Flanders and Swann Musicals fame) and his friend David Marsh had approached Jack with the idea of setting Jack's book *Perelandra* as an opera. David had agreed to write the libretto and Donald the music. How did Jack feel about it? He responded positively; and on 14 July 1960 the three of them met at The Kilns for breakfast followed by a stroll around the garden, discussing the opera for about an hour. Jack then asked to be excused, pointing out that his wife had died the night before. Donald Swann was deeply impressed by Jack's courtesy to them in such circumstances. The work was eventually produced and brought Jack real pleasure.

During the month of August, Bill Gresham came to visit his boys and met with Jack several times. Bill eventually took cancer of the tongue and throat. Sadly, he died of an overdose of sleeping pills at the Dixie Hotel in New York City in September 1962.[8]

Where to now for the bridegroom and widower? He turned again to that great solace in his life, writing. He poured his grief into ink, and out of that grief came an extraordinary book. In the month following Joy's death, Jack wrote *A Grief Observed*. He did not initially set out to publish his writing about his grief, but in September he showed the manuscript to Roger Lancelyn Green and they discussed the possibility of publishing it. He wanted it to be of help to other grieving people. The manuscript was submitted to Faber, one of whose directors was the poet T. S. Eliot. Like multitudes of others, he found the work incredibly moving. In four short parts, Jack poignantly faced what his grief was doing to him. Here were the raw emotions of a man torn apart by bereavement with its doubts and fears. Jack tells honestly of how he went looking for God, but found the door slammed in his face, followed by silence.

It is his most personal work, even more personal than *Surprised by Joy*; and it reveals the depths of his feelings for Joy Gresham. He rages at God as Job did. And, like Job, he slowly and eventually turns to the great Creator and begins to praise the One who had made his wife. The cries of agony in this work are potent, but there is healing in its lines, and a dawning understanding that grief is a process, and that it is useless to speculate about it. In the end, the best is perhaps what we least understand. In their despair, untold multitudes of grieving people have found *A Grief Observed* to be a source of inspiration and relief. There is not a platitude or a cliché to be found anywhere. The book may be a dissection of grief, but it leads on to the great truth of Christian hope. Just within these last few weeks, I have talked to two very different people, one an academic and one a comedienne, both living in Ulster, who found invaluable help in *A Grief Observed.*

It is entirely understandable that Jack felt he could not publish this book under his own name. It was too personal, and it might embarrass his friends. Also, he was sure that it would bring mail that would overwhelm him. Imagine his surprise when the book was published under a pseudonym and he received copies from people who hoped it would help him in his grief! He said nothing about his authorship.

A Grief Observed was published in 1961, under the pseudonym N. W. Clerk ("N. W." was an abbreviation of *Nat Whilk*, Anglo-Saxon for "I not know whom"), but did not sell well until it was reissued in 1964 under Lewis's own name.

Is there a lesson in this pattern? I remember when as a young Christian, I was beginning to write for the cause of Christ's kingdom. When I saw my name on the cover of my first book, I wondered at the propriety of it. Should I write anonymously? I went to see a wise friend, and he said, "Well, Paul did not have a problem with it, did he? He began all of his letters with his name." Of course, what he said was true. Paul didn't even wait until the end of his letters to declare his authorship! "Let your name stand for something," my friend counselled.

A Grief Observed published under the name of N. W. Clerk did not signify as much as it did when the world discovered it was actually C. S. Lewis observing grief. By God's grace, his name and kindness had come to stand for something. C. S. Lewis's name proves it is not true to say that no one is irreplaceable.

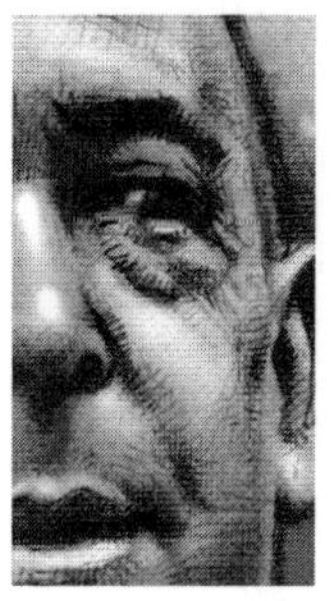

Chapter Eighteen

A SHIVER OF WONDER

Autumn was Jack's favourite season. He called it the best of all seasons. He once wrote to a friend that he wasn't sure if old age wasn't the best part of life, except that, like autumn, it didn't last.

In October 1960, the beeches of England were in their full October glory of gold, russet, and amber. Keats called autumn "the close-bosomed friend of the maturing sun." He was right, for autumn sunshine is mellow. As the month passed, millions of leaves began to fall in masses of crimson and gold. In the meadows there were hoards of mushrooms and toadstools, and fungus growth had reached its peak. The violet-blue bloom of sloes was visible, as was the vivid scarlet provided by the guelder rose. The hawthorn bushes carried a multitude of crimson haws, and the wild roses were loaded with hips.

Across England, the crab apple trees carried good crops of the little sour green or yellow apples. Boys could be seen throwing sticks into the horse chestnut trees to dislodge the fruit. Grey squirrels were scrambling around the bases of the hazel bushes in search of nuts, or out on the meadows collecting fallen acorns. On finding an acorn, they sat up on their haunches, holding the acorn in their forepaws and nibbling at it, and then popped it right into their mouths. They would then bound towards the base of a nearby hedge, looking for a suitable spot to dig a hole, bury the acorn, cover it, and then pat the earth down flat. Any acorns that they did not dig up in the coming winter would reappear the next year as seedlings of the mighty oak.

During autumn, there was one little song that started the day and rang out again after dusk had fallen. It was the silvery trill and warble of the home-keeping English robin.

There is a phenomenon in British weather that is one of the most fascinating features of its climate. It is called the Indian Summer. It is a period of dry, warm weather that sometimes occurs in late autumn. It consists of mild, sunny, misty days that are more like the first warm days of early spring than they are like days of autumn.

Jack Lewis was in the autumn of his significant life; but he was enjoying an Indian Summer, bursting with activity. On 6 October 1960, he travelled from Cambridge to London and spent the night at the Athenaeum Club on Pall Mall. The Athenaeum is a club for individuals who are known for their scientific, literary, or aristocratic associations, and it has had a long association with Anglican dignitaries. Anthony Trollope worked on his novels at the Club; and Jack must have felt at home as he walked through the entrance, with the Club's cipher bearing the Greek letters *Alpha, Beta, Gamma, Delta* within a mosaic wreath on the floor. Nearby, there stood a classical statue of Apollo. Jack had his mind on something more important than the literature of Greece, though. Next morning, he went to Lambeth Palace to attend a committee on the revision of the Psalms. He enjoyed this work and also the stimulating conversation with the committee members.

Jack began his twice-weekly lectures "English Literature between 1300 and 1500" at Cambridge University. Even at the time he was writing *A Grief Observed,* he was also working on a short book which was to prove to be an outstanding work of literary criticism. In a nutshell, the book described the problem of how literary critics can come between readers and good books. Jack felt that literature exists for the joy of the reader, and that, in reading great literature the reader should transcend himself, for he was never more himself than when he did this. He maintained that English literature was not primarily an academic subject. Jack wanted to preserve the main experience of the reader as being above education.

When Jack was asked to comment on undergraduate criticism published in the little Cambridge *Broadsheet,* he did not equivocate. He showed how criticism from undergraduates is but an imitation of their elders. In October 1960, in a Cambridge undergraduate literary magazine called *Delta,* the undergraduates responded with vengeance, bad manners, and bitterness in heavy measure. Jack's assertion that most English literature was composed for adult readers who knew the Bible and the classics, had added fuel to their flame.

The controversy spread to the Cambridge University newspaper *Variety,* and thence to *The Listener, The Times Literary Supplement*, and *The Spectator*. Professor F. R. Leavis took the undergraduates' side. If ever a man had put his head above the parapet, Jack Lewis was that man. Despite a heart breaking from grief, his passion for literature and for introducing others to its joys remained undiminished. Defiantly and brilliantly, he defended the "castle of literature" for the reader, against the critic.

The New Year saw Jack hard at work on a new twice-weekly series of lectures on Edmund Spenser's *Faerie Queene*. The booming voice, the mirth in his eyes, the passion for his subject, the carefully chosen illustrations, the gifted articulation that had gripped many English Literature undergraduates at Oxford, now gripped the undergraduates at Cambridge. Work also continued on the Commission to Revise the Psalter. On 23 February, Jack gave a memorable talk on Samuel Pepys at Magdalene College at the annual dinner to celebrate Pepys' birthday. Jack was also collecting and revising his poems, with a view to having them published.

In his *Life of C. S. Lewis*, Walter Hooper highlights a very poignant piece of writing from Jack that arrived on the desk of Jocelyn Gibb, the Managing Director of Jeffrey Bles (the firm that was publishing the Narnian stories). Jocelyn had been greatly used to encourage Jack in his writing. Jack had been working on a collection of essays for publication, and had written a new passage for transposition to his book. The passage was a sermon he had preached on 28 May at Mansfield College, the youngest and smallest of Oxford's thirty-nine colleges. It was about heaven, a subject that always brought the best out of Jack.[1]

It is hard now to realise that it was only by an Act of Parliament in 1871 that the educational and social opportunities offered by Britain's premier institutions were made available to all Non-conformists. To his eternal credit, it was the British Prime Minister W. E. Gladstone who first recommended that a Non-conformist college be founded at Oxford. Mansfield College moved from Birmingham to Oxford in 1886. The College occupies one of the most attractive sites in Oxford; and its beautiful chapel is a fine setting for any sermon on Heaven. Jack's sermon tackled the problem we all have in thinking of Heaven in negative terms: no food, no events, no time, no art, etc.

Jack created a fable in which he imagined a boy being brought up by his mother in a dungeon. All the boy knows of the outside world are the pictures of it that his mother draws for him. Suddenly, the mother realises that her child thinks the real world is full of lines drawn in lead pencil. When he is told it isn't, his whole notion of the world outside his dungeon becomes a blank. Jack said that it is so with our concept of heaven. The "pencil lines" of our experience will vanish in the real landscape of resurrection life. The candlelight of our experience will become invisible when the window blind is pulled up and the risen sun blazes in. Jack believed that history shows that the Christians who did most for this present world were those who thought most of the next one. Little did he realise how significantly he was one of those Christians. Heaven was no bribe for him any more than a man's love for a woman is mercenary because he wants to marry her. Love seeks to enjoy its object; and he was looking forward to seeing God. For those who did not want God, there was Hell. That was the place where God left you if you didn't want Him. For Jack, though, his great goal of seeing God was nearer than he thought.

Somehow, for me, the stage I have now reached in this biography is the most difficult part to write. Here was a man who, as we have just seen, was at the very height of his writing powers. After all the pains and pleasures, the joys and sorrows of his long pilgrimage, he had come now to a point where he was matured and full of wisdom from life's varied experiences. His inability as a child to hold scissors and create a castle from cardboard had led Jack to hold a pen and from his informed mind, awesomely, to create much more than castles. He had almost become a household name in the English-speaking world. His fame had not affected his humanity in the slightest, as his letters patently show. This fact is demonstrated particularly in the book published in 1967 by Wm. B. Eerdmans entitled *Letters to an American Lady*. In 1950, Jack had begun a correspondence with an American lady whom he would never meet. These letters reveal the generous and compassionate side of his nature. Over the last thirteen years of his life, he patiently offered encouragement and guidance to another human being in the day-to-day joys and sorrows of life. Life's impermanence, as well as the fact that *here we have no abiding city*, was now about to be demonstrated in Jack's own experience. His dear friend Arthur Greeves, with whom he had a glorious reunion in Oxford in late June 1961, noted that Jack looked very ill. Sadly, it was all too true.

After Arthur had gone home to Belfast, Jack went to see his own doctor and friend Robert Harvard, who diagnosed an enlarged prostate gland. His surgeon eventually decided that Jack was not fit enough to withstand an operation. His kidneys were infected, and he was suffering from toxemia. His heart had also been affected, and he was experiencing cardiac irregularities. At this stage, he had to sleep upright in a chair at night. He was unable to go back to Cambridge for the Michaelmas Term of 1961, and stayed at home with Warren, David, and Douglas. He also began having a series of blood transfusions at the Ackland Nursing Home. These treatments led to a gradual and continuing improvement in his condition between June 1962 and July 1963.

During his illness, Jack's friends were a great source of help and encouragement to him. Quite a few of them visited him at The Kilns. On Mondays he still went to The Eagle and Child, and often on to The Trout at Godstow for lunch. On Wednesday mornings he took communion with his local parish minister, Ronald Head, at The Kilns. He began to re-read some of his favourite books, including Tolstoy's *War and Peace*, Merton's *No Man is an Island*, Wordsworth's *The Prelude*, Ruskin's *Praeterila* and *Modern Painters*. He also read the *Odyssey* and *Iliad* in Greek, and the *Aeneid* in Latin. He read again works by Jane Austen, Charles Dickens, Anthony Trollope, Sir Walter Scott, and George Herbert. As ever, his pen kept flowing. He began to write the book "behind" his lecture series "The Prolegomena to Medieval and Renaissance Literature." It was published in 1964 as *The Discarded Image*. The review in the *Times Literary Supplement* of 10 July 1964 said that the book "represents Lewis the expositor at his best, and communicates the zest that he brought to the study of literature, philosophy and religion alike."

The zest for the things that he cared for never left Jack. Sometimes, the impression is given that as he came towards the end of his life he was filled with doubt, and that his once-surging faith had diminished. The claim simply is not true.

In April 1962, Jack returned to Cambridge University to resume his twice-weekly lectures on *The Faerie Queene*. Jack's friend George Sayer tells of taking him on that return journey to Cambridge, and stopping at the Woburn Estate. They slipped in through a little gate into the woods. As Jack sat in a glade watching the small deer, he told George that when he was writing the Narnia stories he had never imagined anything as lovely.[2] Next time they stopped at Woburn though, the deer were gone, and the entrancing beauty had passed.

In the summer of 1962, Jack finished his book *The Discarded Image*, and was given an Honorary Doctorate by the University of Dijon. Jack now had quiet, peaceful days; but they were shattered in September by the suicide of Bill Gresham. It caused Jack great pain to have to pass on the sad news to Douglas and David.

Jack returned to Cambridge in October to resume his lectures, "English Literature 1300-1500." They were to be his last. In November, Tolkien invited him to a special dinner in connection with his seventieth birthday, but Jack did not feel able to attend because of the restrictions his illness had put upon him. Tolkien and Lewis corresponded that Christmas, the old love and respect for each other as deep as ever. Tolkien visited Jack twice in 1962 and 1963.

For some time Jack had wanted to write a book on prayer, but it had not worked out. He made an attempt, but it had faltered because he had not found a suitable genre in which to express his thinking. He finally abandoned the work until early in 1963, when the idea came to him to write about prayer in an imaginary series of letters to a friend. Unbeknownst to Jack, it was to be his last book. It was called *Letters to Malcolm*.[3] It is touching that the last of his twenty-two letters finishes on the great Bible quotation regarding the future state of the believer beyond death: *For we know that we shall be like Him, for we shall see Him as He is*.[4]

The New Year brought Jack yet another honorary doctorate, this time from the University of Lyon. He continued his work at Cambridge, and before Easter he contacted Arthur Greeves about another visit home. Arthur felt that a visit to Donegal would be too exhausting, so they decided to go somewhere along the North Coast of Northern Ireland. It was to be back to those wide, pale skies of his childhood at Castlerock. Jack decided to take Douglas with him to help carry his luggage. He was really looking forward to the trip, well aware that it could be his last.

If I were a film director and filming the life of C. S. Lewis, towards the end I would roll my cameras across the lawn and garden of a beautiful English country home in Cirencester, set in June 1963. The occasion to be enacted would be the first performance of the opera in three acts of Jack's *Perelandra*. Six years after that first performance, after it had been performed in New York on 2 November 1969, the *New Yorker* published a review: "It is a genuine opera, with a very serious plot, and it is full of arias and has a deft score....The idiom of the music is, as most progressive composers would say, 'not of our time.' It is unabashedly old-fashioned. It represents the Handel-Mendelssohn tradition, which is the tradition of most unselfconscious British Music" (6 December 1969).

Not of our time? At the opera's heart there were things that are eternal. In fact, to be relevant we need to say things that are eternal. Singing at the piano with others at that first performance was Donald Swann. Donald had pursued a life-long quest of religious faith and doubt. As a student at Christ Church Oxford, he had written serious settings of the works of poets such as Pushkin, Froissart, and Ronsard.

The man seeking faith but plagued with doubt had found something in the writing of C. S. Lewis that touched him. Listening to Donald singing, that same C. S. Lewis, "apostle to the sceptics," has tears flowing down his cheeks. He is moved by what Donald Swann and David Marsh have done with his work. The performance is like a microcosm of Jack's ministry, reaching to "the man on the outside."

Sixteen days later, on the very day he was to have left for his holiday in Northern Ireland, Jack had a heart attack and went into a coma. The next day he regained consciousness and eventually was sent home to The Kilns on 6 August. He had a male nurse called Alec Ross who cared for him, as well as Mrs. Maude Millar the housekeeper and his newly appointed secretary, Walter Hooper. The faithful Paxford, too, was still looking after The Kilns.

Where was Warren? Jack had received a note from the hospital of Our Lady of Lourdes in Drogheda, to say that they had taken him in. His drinking problem was as severe as ever. George Sayer volunteered to go to Ireland and find out the situation. When he got there, the medical authorities told him that Warren was not fit to travel at present, and they undertook to break the news of Jack's condition to him gently. Warren was able to return to the Kilns in September. As the end of Jack's life drew near, he and Warren became close once more.

Tolkien and his son Christopher visited Jack for the last time in the autumn of 1963; and the old passionate love of literature was as deep as ever between these two giants. They talked of Sir Thomas Malory's fifteenth-century *Le Morte d' Arthur*, which contains timeless champions of the helpless, and assumes the recognition of a loftier standard of justice, purity, and unselfishness than was known in its own century. The book exudes knightly honour, courtly love, and chivalric duty. Did they discuss how the legend tells of King Arthur being taken away on a boat as he was dying? Would it not have been priceless to hear them have their last conversation? They talked for an hour.

On 14 October 1963, Jack's retirement was announced in the *Times*.

> Professor C. S. Lewis has resigned, because of ill health, his appointment as Professor of Medieval and Renaissance English at Cambridge, and his Fellowship at Magdalene College....He said he could be driven in a car, but he could not walk more than a short distance, and was unable to climb stairs. "It could be very much worse; at least it does not hurt like toothache," he said....He is now correcting the proofs of *The Discarded*

> *Image*—"A sort of background to medieval literature," he said. "I always have a hundred major projects in mind. It is nice to have leisure, and I may be able to get down to all those books I have never written."

"All those books I have never written"? It was not an idle mind that was approaching death, but a richly fertile one. Who knows what further works of inspiration would have flowed from his heart and mind if he had lived? But God had other plans for Jack. As he faced the prospect of death, he told his brother that he had done all he wanted to do, and that he was ready to go. This statement showed great contentment and peace of mind; but if he were to live he clearly did not intend to be idle.

As 22 November 1963 dawned, it was a day to be remembered across the world. On that day Lee Harvey Oswald allegedly lifted a high-powered rifle and shot President John F. Kennedy from a window in the Texas School Book Depository. Annually, two million people visit Dealy Plaza, which the President rode along on that fateful day. That slaying was a defining moment in my teenage years; and like hundreds of millions of others I can remember where I was when I heard about it. Etched into our minds are the rider-less horse in the President's funeral possession, the salute of his little son, John John, and the black veil across Jacqueline Kennedy's face. John F. Kennedy had hardly passed his first one thousand days in office. Naturally, the death of this President of Irish descent occupied the minds of the world on that horrendous day.

The Professor of Irish descent arose that morning and had his breakfast. He then attended to his letters and worked on the day's crossword puzzle. After lunch, he fell asleep in his chair, and Warren suggested that he would be more comfortable in his bed. He agreed, and at 4.00 p.m., in a timeworn tradition, Warren took him a cup of tea. They had a few words together, and Warren left him drowsy but comfortable.

At 5.30 p.m. Warren heard a crash and ran to the room to find Jack lying unconscious at the foot of his bed. Three or four minutes later he left this Shadowlands to meet *The Lion of the Tribe of Judah, the King of all kings and the Lord of all lords.*

On 26 November 1963, a cold but sunlit day, his funeral was held at his parish church, Holy Trinity, Headington. His close friends gathered for the service. Amongst them were Lady Dunbar, née Maureen Moore, Professor J. R. R. Tolkien, Dr. Harvard, Miss Wakeham, the President and Vice-President of Magdalen College and Inklings, J. H. Dundas-Grant, Owen Barfield, A. C. Harwood, George Sayer, and Austin Farrer. There, too, was the faithful Paxford. Warren had the words "Men must endure their going hence" cut into Jack's tombstone; they were the words to be found on the Shakespeare Calendar the day their mother died.

Never have I found a book so hard to finish. Where can one finally lay down his pen on such a mind and life? As we part, my reader, would you allow me one more musing? If you have stayed with me this length of time, you will be aware that I have been trying to show the deep influence that Ulster had upon C. S. Lewis. It is to this Province that I now wish to return and refer to something once said to me by a man who lives here. He'd worked for a pharmacist and had not gone to the pharmacist's funeral. Here is the story:

One of the leading pharmacists in an Ulster town,
He was the conduit of suffering.
Colds, flu, ulcers, earaches, headaches,
Sore throats, upset stomachs, upset-most-things,

Found ease and even cures through his hands,
And he was generous and kind.
Even those who could not afford their prescriptions
Were not refused his skills, pills, and knowledge.
For years he was at the heart of his community.
"I should have been at his funeral,"
The man told the pharmacist's wife with embarrassment,
Because he had worked for him as a boy.
"I thought there would have been lots of people there."
"There were three," she replied.
He turned to me with a word of revelation:
"When ministers say at large funerals,
'The crowd here today represents
How great a person this was,
How well respected in the community,'
They are lying," he said.

Was not the man right?
A life is never truly represented by a crowd.

I reckon that fewer than fifty people turned up at C. S. Lewis's funeral service. Even Warren didn't make it. The *Times* mentions twenty-two by name. Yet the Ulsterman got it right: ultimately it is not in a crowd that a man's greatness is represented, for crowds are fickle. The important thing is what endures from a life. Millions upon millions of people have recognised what endures from the life of C. S. Lewis. What, then, is his enduring legacy? What has he given to us? Lots of things! Yet, what he has given is ultimately that *shiver of wonder* we get at times when we read his writing. He enables us to see beyond it, to the living God he is writing about. He makes us look away to the time when the term is over, and the holidays really have begun; when the dream has finally ended and we have arrived at the eternal morning; when the vista won't be Belfast Lough and the Holywood Hills, or Carlingford Lough and the Cooley or Mourne Mountains. Rather the vista will be of that celestial shore, into which Jack has already helped give us more than an inkling.

END NOTES

PREFACE

1. The Listener, 72 (16th July 1964), p.97.
2. See 1 Corinthians 14:23.
3. *Just as I am*, Billy Graham, Harper Collins Publishers, 1997, p.224-225.
4. "God's Funeral," Hardy, *Collected Poems*, p.307
5. Lubbock, p.259.
6. "Christian Apologetics," quoted by Walter Hooper in *C. S. Lewis: A Companion and Guide*, Harper Collins, 1996, p.30.
7. *Jack: A life of C. S. Lewis*, George Sayer, Hodder and Stoughton, 1997, p.282.
8. Walden Media, New York, 31st July 2002.
9. *The Dairies of Kenneth Tynan*, edited by John Lahr, Bloomsbury, 2001, pp.194-5.
10. Ibid, pp.405-6.
11. Ibid, p.37.
12. Ibid, p.322.
13. *The Path To Power*, Margaret Thatcher, Harper Collins Publishers, 1955, p.40.
14. *The Horse and His Boy*, p.11.
15. The Song of Solomon 1: 3; 4:10.

CHAPTER 1

1. 2 Samuel 23:4.
2. *The Belfast and Province of Ulster Directory for 1905*: Ref 244, PRONI. Compiled by The Belfast News Letter Office. Copyright secured at Stationary Hall, London.
3. *Belfast, An Illustrated*, Jonathan Bardon, The Blackstaff Press Ltd., 1982, p.156.
4. *Jack*, George Sayer, Hodder and Stoughton, 1997, p.42.
5. *Surprised by Joy*, Inspirational Press, by arrangement with Harcourt Brace Jovanovich Inc., 1991, p.11.

6. *Ibid*, p.11.
7. 2 Corinthians 12:2-4, *The Message*. Copyright Eugene H. Peterson, 1993, 1994, 1995. Used by permission of NavPress Publishing Group.

CHAPTER 2

1. *Surprised by Joy*, Inspirational Press, by arrangement with Harcourt Brace Jovanovich Inc, 1991, p.8.
2. Romans 8:28.
3. *The Lewis Papers: Memoirs of the Lewis Family, 1850-1930* (eleven volumes), Leeborough Press. A typescript of the original is in the Wade Collection, Wheaton, Illinois.
4. *Light on C. S. Lewis*, "The Approach to English", ed. Jocelyn Gibb, London, Geoffrey Bles, 1965, p.64.

CHAPTER 3

1. *Jack*, George Sayer, Hodder and Stoughton, 1997, p.57.
2. *Nicholas Nickleby*, Wordsworth Classics, 2000, p.148.
3. *The Last Battle*, Fontana, 1980, p.173.

CHAPTER 4

1. *The Times*, February 20th 2004.
2. Permission to quote from the *C. S. Lewis News* given by James O'Fee, former Chairman of the C. S. Lewis Centenary Group, which is now dissolved.
3. From *Representative Poetry Online*, A UTEL (University of Toronto English Library) Edition.
4. *Ibid*.
5. *The Poems*, Matthew Arnold, Oxford University Press, 1930, p.401.

CHAPTER 5

1. *W. B. Yeats and His World*, Thames and Hudson, London, 1971, p.30.
2. *Ibid*, pp.27-29.
3. *Surprised by Joy*, Inspirational Press, by arrangement with Harcourt Brace Jovanovich Inc, 1991, p.34.
4. Quoted in *Parents and Teenagers*, Victor Books, a division of SP Publications, Inc., 1984, p.316.
5. *The Desert Wings*, 3rd March 1978, AFFTC, History Office.
6. *Jack*, A Life of C. S. Lewis, George Sayer, Hodder and Stoughton, 1997, pp.67-68.

7. Ibid, p.68.
8 *Surprised by Joy,* Inspirational Press, by arrangement with Harcourt Brace Jovanovich Inc., 1991, p.41.

CHAPTER 6

1. Quotation taken from an essay on James Hilton on the *Exxon Mobil Masterpiece Theatre* website.
2. *The Collected Poems of Wilfred Owen,* edited by C. Day Lewis, Chatto and Windus Ltd., 1963, p.31.
3. *Ibid.,* p.44.

CHAPTER 7

1. Source, *George MacDonald, Scotland's Beloved Storyteller,* Michael R. Phillips, Bethany House Publishers, Minneapolis, Minnesota, 1987, p.335. Mr. Phillips gives his source for this poem as Greville MacDonald, *op.cit.,* p.559-560.

CHAPTER 8

1. *Surprised by Joy,* Inspirational Press, by arrangement with Harcourt Brace and Javanovic Inc., 1991, p.86.
2. See *Narnian Ulster* by Mary Rodgers on the C. S. Lewis Centenary Group website.
3. A scutcher was involved in the dressing of retted flax by beating it.
4. In the local dialect "oul" means "old"; "wheen," a "lot"; and "axed" means "asked"
5. *Livin' in Drumlister,* The Collected Ballads and Verses of W. F. Marshall, The Blackstaff Press Limited, 1983, p.50.
6. *The Pilgrim's Regress,* C. S. Lewis, Fount paperbacks, William Collins Sons & Co. Ltd., 1977, p.6-7.

CHAPTER 10

1. Quoted in Violets from Oversea, by Tonie and Valmai Holt, Leo Cooper, 1996, p.219.
2. Ibid, page 211.
3. Ibid, page 143.
4. See 1 Kings chapter 10.

CHAPTER 11

1. *Surprised by Joy,* Inspirational Press, by arrangement with Harcourt Brace Jovanovich Inc., 1991.
2. Acts 10:43.
3. *Letters of C. S. Lewis,* Edited, with a memoir by W. H. Lewis, Fount, An Imprint of HarperCollins Publishers,1988.
4. 1 John 4:14, 15; 5:10-12.
5. Matthew 7:13, 14.

CHAPTER 12

1. *A Witch's Brewing,* F. W. Boreham, The Epworth Press, London, 1932, p.27-28.
2. *The Pilgrim's Regress,* Collins, Fount Paperbacks, 1977.
3. *Ibid.,* p.216.
4. Matthew 10:39.
5. *Jack, A Life of* C. S. Lewis, George Sayer, Hodder and Stoughton, 1997, p.226.
6. *The Pilgrim's Regress,* Collins, Fount Paperbacks, 1977, p.216.
7. Proverbs 27:19.
8. Quoted in *C. S. Lewis, A Companion and Guide,* Walter Hooper, Fount, An Imprint of Harper Collins Publishers, 1997, p.25.
9. *The Problem of Pain,* Collins, Fontana Books, 1957.

CHAPTER 13

1. *The Peverel Papers,* Flora Thompson, Century Hutchinson, 1986, p.181-182.
2. *Fern-seed and Elephants,* C. S. Lewis, Fontana, 1975, p.26-38.
3. 1 Corinthians 10:31.
4. Hebrews 13:14.
5. Matthew 5:39.
6. *Christian Counter-Culture,* J. R. W. Stott, IVP, 1979, p.108.
7. *Ibid.,* p.108-109.
8. *Jack,* George Sayer, Hodder and Stoughton, 1997, p.311.
9. James 4:7.
10. Quoted in *C. S. Lewis at the BBC,* Justin Phillips, Harper Collins Publishers, 2002, p.51-52.
11. Quoted in *The Caged Lion, Winston Spencer Churchill, 1932-1940,* William Manchester, Cardinal, 1988, p.686.
12. Foreword by J. W. Welch, to Dorothy L. Sayers' *The Man Born To Be King,* Victor Gollancz, London, 1943, p.11ff .
13. *BBC Handbook,* 1942, p.59.

CHAPTER 14

1. "Common Decency" by C. S. Lewis, Fellow of Magdalen College, Oxford.
2. Esther 4:14.
3. *The Cross of Christ*, John Stott, IVP, p.334.
4. *Ibid.*, p336-337.
5. *C. S. Lewis at the BBC,* Justin Phillips, Harper Collins Publishers, 2002, p.151.
6. *Ibid.*, p.297.
7. John 4:14.
8. Matthew 24:22.
9. Genesis 11:1-9.
10. *That Hideous Strength,* C. S. Lewis, Pan Books, 1955, p.13.
11. A. C. Scupholme, *Theology L,* (October 1947), pp.395-7.
12. From *St. Andrews Citizen*, 29th June 1946.

CHAPTER 15

1. *Northern Ireland,* text by Ian Hill, The Blackstaff Press, published with the assistance of the IDB, 1986, p.62.
2. See *C. S. Lewis: A Companion and Guide,* Walter Hooper, Fount, An Imprint of Harper Collins Publishers, 1997, pp. 64, 92.
3. *The Horse and His Boy,* C. S. Lewis, Collins, An imprint of Harper Collins Publishers, 2001, p.180.
4. Psalm 34:19.
5. Quoted in *C. S. Lewis: A Companion and Guide,* Walter Hooper, Fount, An imprint of Harper Collins Publishers, 1997, p.36-37. These thoughts were originally written down by Lady Freud for Stephen Schofield to use in his book, *In Search of C. S. Lewis* (1983).
6. Isaiah 40:29-31.
7. Romans 8:28.
8. *The Oxford Magazine* LXX111, Review by J.B.L., 2nd December 1954, p.134.
9. Commander of the British Empire.
10. *C. S. Lewis, Letters,* Edited by W. H. Lewis, Fount, An imprint of Harper Collins Publishers, 1988, p.40.

CHAPTER 16

1. *These Found the Way: Thirteen Converts to Protestant Christianity,* Ed. David Wesley Soper, Philadelphia, The Westminster Press, 1951, pp.15-16.
2. *C. S. Lewis, A Companion and Guide,* Walter Hooper, Hodder and Stoughton, 1996, p.77.

CHAPTER 17

1. *C. S. Lewis, Letters,* Fount, An Imprint of HarperCollins Publishers, 1988, p.470.
2. Ibid., p.44-45.
3. Ibid., p.466.
4. Ibid., p.44-45.
5. Ibid., p.474.
6. *The Four Loves,* Collins, Fount Paperbacks, 1977.
7. *Reflections on the Psalms,* Inspirational Press, by arrangement with Harcourt, Brace Jovanovich Inc., 1991.
8 *C. S. Lewis, A Companion and Guide,* Fount, An imprint of HarperCollins Publishers, p.96.

CHAPTER 18

1. *C. S. Lewis, A Companion and Guide,* Walter Hooper, Fount, An Imprint of HarperCollins Publishers, p.108-109.
2. *Jack, A life of C. S. Lewis,* George Sayer, Hodder and Stoughton, 1997, p.402.
3. First published by Geoffrey Bles in 1964.
4. 1 John 3:2.
5. Called druggist in the United States.

The author wishes to thank his typist, Dorothy, for her patient and dedicated work in typing the manuscript for this book. She professes to have found the life of C. S. Lewis to be a truly inspiring journey.